JOYCE RUPP

God's
ENDURING
PRESENCE

Strength for the spiritual journey

D1023880

TWENTY
THIRD 23rd
PUBLICATIONS
www.23rdpublications.com

TWENTY-THIRD PUBLICATIONS
A Division of Bayard
One Montauk Avenue, Suite 200
New London, CT 06320
(860) 437-3012 or (800) 321-0411
www.23rdpublications.com

ISBN 978-1-58595-720-0
Library of Congress Catalog Card Number: 2008939038
Printed in the U.S.A.

Contents

EASTER TO PENTECOST

FESTIVALS

ORDINARY TIME

Introduction

As I reviewed the reflections contained in this book, I noticed that quite a few directly or indirectly focus on the presence of God. This did not surprise me but it did reawaken me to how my awareness of the Holy One's nearness has claimed my heart. This dimension of my faith has nurtured and sustained my life since childhood. As I have aged, much has changed in both my external and internal world. One thing that has not been altered is my consistent experience of the enduring quality of God's presence. Through the joys and sorrows of my years, this abiding love remains strong and lasting. I cannot imagine my life without the treasure of the Holy One's steadfast companionship and guidance.

A long time ago, when I read the revelations of the mystic, Julian of Norwich, I resonated with her statement that "God is nearer to us than our own soul." Her belief in God's enduring presence was founded on her intimate closeness with divinity. In *Revelations of Divine Love*, Julian writes: "Our soul is so deeply grounded in God and so endlessly treasured that we cannot come to the knowing of it until we have first come to the knowing of God, who is the maker to whom it is joined."

This loving "joining" with our Creator sustains my life. Experience of God's presence happens in varied forms and times. One word or phrase from Scripture can leap out and draw me into spending time with the whisper of truth calling to me. In this brief moment of "recognition" I see that this stirring comes not from my human consciousness but from a deeper place

1

where Wisdom dwells within me. At other times, I am in conversation with a loved one, or sometimes with a stranger, and I become aware of a movement of kindness kindling my heart. Again, I have a sense that this Love is larger and fuller than my own.

I have known the presence of divinity in meaningful worship when I've gathered with others to sing a rousing song of praise or been deeply moved by reception of the Eucharist. I've especially been aware of God's companionship when I am in nature. Something as simple as the full moon rising or the sight of a fledgling bird learning to fly connects me with the Creator in an inspiring moment of awe.

Daily prayer and meditation are central ways in which I have maintained my awareness and gratitude for God's enduring presence. This is why I readily responded "yes" when first asked many years ago to write brief reflections on the daily Scripture readings for Creative Communications' *Living Faith* publication. My positive decision arose from a desire to help others grow in both attentiveness and appreciation of the Holy One's nearness.

The short essays found within these pages have been edited but they are basically the ones I've written for *Living Faith* during the past seven years. (A previous collection of reflections can be found in my book, *Inviting God In.*) As you use these reflections for your prayer, may they enrich your faith and draw you ever closer to our Enduring Presence.

Advent

I Need "Doses of Encouragement"

The desert and the parched land will exult.

ISAIAH 35:1

Advent Scripture passages are marvelous messengers of hope. I enjoy this liturgical season more than any other. Each day these readings offer me a fresh opportunity to have my hope reawakened. I envision Advent as a time of allowing my spirit to soak in the scriptural promises and pledges. This season invites me to look around and notice how God moves amid my life each day as an advocate of hope through the positive people and encouraging situations I encounter.

During Advent I try to retune my attitudes, to see where I am stuck in life's obstacles and dissatisfactions. As I do, I uncover places in me that need a good dose of encouragement. In spite of my having a positive outlook, it's amazing how quickly life's troubles affect my spirit. Advent Scriptures daily remind me to regain my spiritual balance. Like a parched land exulting with new life or a deluge of rain causing a dry desert to bloom with flowers, my arid hope comes alive. I discover again that what I want to give up on actually holds the potential for future blooming and blessing.

 God of Hope, seek out the places of my heart that are parched and dry. Refresh my spirit with renewed trust in your love.

A Time to Firm Up My Foundation

But it did not collapse; it had been set solidly on rock.

MATTHEW
7:25

The house I live in is quite old. The structure constantly needs some work. Recently, the floor of the pantry closet had to be replaced, including the boards beneath the tile, because the wood had rotted and was slowly crumbling—the very foundation was giving way. The deteriorating floor reminded me that Advent is a season to look at my foundation of love, to see if it remains solid or is crumbling and in need of some attention and repair.

While many complain of the busyness of this season and the huge amount of "to do's" that are a part of it, I do think there is an "upside" to this overly active time. When I am unstressed and unrushed, being a nice, caring person poses little trouble for me. The challenge to my kindness and caring occurs when my life swells to stressful proportions and I feel like screaming at everybody. That's when the mettle of my Christianity is really tested. So when the Advent days get boggled with activity and pressure, I try to approach it as an good opportunity to turn frustration and impatience into golden bricks of kindness, a time to strengthen my foundation of union with the One who is the source of all love.

 God of patience, hold my hand and guide me toward kindness as I move among the fullness of the day.

Gift-Giving That Makes a Difference

Open to me the gates of justice; I will enter them and give thanks to the Lord.

PSALM 118:19

Justice requires that all people have a right to basic needs such as food, clothing, and shelter. Yet many do not have these essential things. Christmas gift-giving can be a delightful experience, but I have also found many Christmases painful because I knew I spent money on presents the recipients definitely did not need. I have wondered how I could change my gift-giving to better reflect my care for people of the world who have little.

Recently, I discovered a way to do this. My mailbox is inundated with requests at this time of year. "Opening the gates of justice" now means opening the mail and deciding what kind of gifts I can give to make a difference, not only to my family and friends but to those who need the basics. Countless organizations will accept a donation in the name of a person being gifted. I can also give food to homeless shelters, buy an animal for a family to raise in a developing country, or send books to children who have no libraries in their schools. I sometimes give "regular" gifts but more and more of my Christmas presents are ones that will be of benefit to those who have less materially than my family and friends do.

 God of the Poor, keep my heart close to those who can benefit from my abundance.

7

Learning from Our Fears

> Say to those whose hearts are frightened: Be strong, fear not!
>
> ISAIAH 35:4

Not long ago I was at a retreat center, a safe place of solitude in the Kansas woods. One especially dark night, I went from my little cabin to the main building. With no lights in the forest, my flashlight was essential for following the path. As I walked along, I heard the rustling of unknown creatures in the nearby leaves and my mind started imaging all sorts of possibilities. Fear leapt up in me for a moment but then I laughed to myself, realizing the animals were probably more afraid of me than I was of them.

Fear can be a powerful friend or a formidable foe. Fear keeps us from harm, but more often it keeps us from trusting God at times when we are being stretched toward maturity in our faith. Every time I have been faced with a "life challenge," I have made a list of my fears. I'm always surprised at how long the list is. Those anxieties and worries rarely became realities. Most often my fears have simply served to drag my energy into self-absorption, fretting, and nervousness. No wonder there are so many Scripture texts advising us to be strong and fear not. Trust in God is a must if we are to have peace.

 Spirit of Courage, when fear rises in my heart and threatens my peace, help me to place my trust in you.

Renewing My Hope

They that hope in the Lord will renew their strength...

ISAIAH
40:31

Hope-filled people inspire and boost the enthusiasm of others. They have an ability to lift the disheartened from the pit of discouragement. It's not that hope-filled persons escape life's woes. It's how they respond that makes the difference. With their spiritual roots sunk deep in Enduring Love, they can stand strong in the wild storms of life and not give up. Hope-filled persons reach out wide and far to receive the empowering strength of God that comes in many disguises.

Jesus was a carrier of hope. We are meant to do the same. The world situation being what it is, we are sometimes greatly challenged to believe in personal and world transformation. Hope can quickly flee from our hearts.

Are we hope-filled? How do we keep our hope alive? Not by self-reliance alone. Isaiah reminds us that it is the ones "who hope in the Lord" who renew their strength. We have to go deep to find the endless Source that feeds the river of love and goodness in our hearts. When we do so, we have the courage to go on hoping in spite of what appears dismal. This Advent, let us renew our hope. Let us sink our roots deeper!

 Source of Grace, with you as my constant companion, I can be a bearer of hope in the midst of a troubled world.

The Straight and Narrow

...and lead you on the way you should go.

ISAIAH
48:17

Mythologist Joseph Campbell commented that if we look far ahead on our journey of life and see a straight road neatly mapped out with clear signs showing in which direction to go, we can be sure it's not our road. I laughed when I heard that, but I also felt it was an accurate comment. How often I've had my future programmed for what I wanted it to be and it turned out radically different than I'd imagined.

None of us knows for certain where the road ahead will take us. Sometimes there are big surprises, unexpected curves, deep holes and pitfalls, or surprisingly beautiful vistas. Each day we take another step on our path of life. That's as far as we can know where the road goes.

No wonder Scripture encourages us to seek the guidance of our divine companion. I have made it a practice for years to pray for spiritual guidance every single morning. I count on this assistance. Without it, I can too easily get lost in my ego ambitions and faulty perceptions of how to live. Whether the day's road reveals a smooth or rough pathway, with God giving the directions, I know the journey will take me where I need to go.

 Guide me on my way today, Spirit of Wisdom. Keep my heart united with you as I take each footstep into the unknown territory of my life.

Our Guide through Painful Times

It is I who say to you, "Fear not, I will help you."

ISAIAH
41:13

I received a letter from a woman who experienced a terrible rejection. She was upset and angry, not just at those who had wronged her, but also at the response of her colleagues. She felt they gave her (in her words), "pious counsel," encouraging her to trust God and believe she would find a happy future. She questioned the worth of their helpful offerings and resented their easy solutions.

I understood why she was unable to accept this valid advice at the time. It is almost impossible to believe spiritual wisdom when we are stuck in feelings of anger and bitterness. The first thing to do is to enter these unwanted emotions, listen to their loud voices and discern what they are telling us. We cannot bypass the human response to painful situations. As we tend to these distressful parts of our self, God is there guiding us, helping us move on to a new beginning, even though we may be unaware of this presence.

When we are in the midst of pain, we may feel that we are not able to prevail over it. That is why faith—believing without seeing or knowing—is essential in times of desolation. With faith, we trust and we do not give up.

Compassionate One, when pain of any kind engulfs me, may your strength be there to lead me through it.

11

Offering the Comfort of God

Comfort,
give
comfort
to my
people,
says your
God.

ISAIAH
40:1

When my father died, someone I did not know well sent me a comforting sympathy card. On the front of it was a small lamb held in the arms of the Good Shepherd on whose face was a tender smile. The sender never knew it, but I kept that card close to me for many months as I grieved. That image brought me immense consolation. Whenever I gazed at the lamb embraced by the Good Shepherd, I felt confident that God would not abandon me in my time of loss.

Isaiah reminds us today that God wants to comfort us when we are hurting. Often we receive this divine embrace through human deeds. Compassionate gestures like taking time to send a card, giving generous help with tasks, offering quiet understanding, being a listening presence, and providing faithful companionship are ways that our comforting God wraps us in love through the goodness of another human being.

How can the compassionate Christ touch the lives of others through our gestures of compassion? Let us look around and notice who might be comforted by our gift of compassion this Advent day. Let us reach out and extend the comfort of God to them.

 Good Shepherd, help me to remember that I can be a source of your comforting presence when I am with those who are hurting.

"Come, Lord Jesus, Come!"

Like a fire there appeared the prophet whose words were as a flaming furnace.

SIRACH 48:1

Prophets were not easy people to listen to because their messages seared with admonitions to move out of unloving ways and self-orientation. The prophets tried to get those around them to see the bigger picture, the deeper truth, the fuller sense of God's love. Jesus was rejected and even chased out of his hometown because people did not want to hear his message. He was later hunted down and killed for his prophetic voice. Jesus challenged the acceptable system, rattled the doors of sluggish spirituality. People longed for a savior, but when he came, they rejected him. They wanted someone else, not a person whose words were full of fiery passion requiring a change of mind and heart.

In this Advent season, we often pray for Jesus to come. Do we know what we pray for? We are asking for a prophet who insisted his followers forgive one another and stop judging others harshly. He asked them to accept people of all nations, to seek the riches of God more than material wealth and to do all they could to heal and to bring peace.

Are we ready for this prophet to be among us? Then let us pray with all our hearts: "Come, Lord Jesus, come!"

 Speak your words of truth to my heart, Jesus. I want to change my ways.

13

The Powerful Presence of the Spirit

The holy Spirit will come upon you, and the power of the Most High will overshadow you.

LUKE
1:35

When the angel Gabriel approached Mary of Nazareth and announced to her that she was to be the mother of the Holy One, Mary was deeply troubled. In spite of the angel's encouragement, Mary's heart was filled with fear. She did not understand how the angel's news could be possible and she questioned this message from God. Mary was assured that what was seemingly impossible would be attainable because the Holy Spirit's power would be with her. This message eased her fears and helped her to say "yes." Imagine what Mary discovered about the immense support and courage of the Spirit in that moment of initial doubt and agonizing questions.

We sometimes face puzzling situations in our lives, too. When those challenging times occur, we might also think it is impossible for us to manage what lies before us. We question whether we can do it. But if we turn to the profound truth of our faith, we will find that we are assured of the same message given to Mary: we do not go through a seemingly impossible situation alone. We always have the powerful presence of the Holy Spirit to give us what we need for our life's journey.

 Spirit of Courage, open my mind and heart to receive spiritual strength and daily reassurance from you.

When Welcoming Christ Is Hard...

And how does this happen to me, that the mother of my Lord should come to me?

LUKE
1:43

Elizabeth's utter amazement at the presence of the God-Child in Mary resonates with joy and humility. Her elated response calls us to be equally astounded at everyone who comes into our life because each one is also a bearer of God's presence, although that presence might be hidden from easy recognizance. Every person, no matter how mean or ugly-behaving, no matter how obnoxious or unsavory, no matter how irritating or unkind, has something of God within them, even though the Divine Presence is concealed from our view.

We are undoubtedly aware of people in whom we find it troublesome to welcome the Christ, such as murderers, drug dealers, sexual predators. But in reality, the Christ in those near to us can also be difficult to welcome. This person might be someone who interrupts our TV program or who barges into our workplace with some absurd or unnecessary problem. It might be a spouse who insists on having his way or a telemarketer who won't take "no" for an answer. This person might even be a grandparent who fails to echo Elizabeth's welcoming words when her teenage grandchild comes to visit bearing a pierced tongue and tattooed arms.

 O Divinity in Disguise, open my eyes and heart to welcome you with the joy that Elizabeth welcomed your presence.

Remembering to "Exult in God"

"My heart exults in the Lord."

I SAMUEL 2:1

"My soul proclaims the greatness of the Lord."

LUKE 1:46

Hannah and Mary begin their canticles with similar words, acknowledging all the Holy One has done for them. The voice of wonder and gratitude in these two amazing women is the inner voice I want to keep this Advent. In this season of "counting down the days 'til Christmas," I get trapped in my frenetic world of self-imposed preparations and miss the things for which I need to give thanks. My heart forgets to "exult in God" because I am unaware of so much that is happening. I get caught up in complaining about "how little time there is" to do all the things I hope to do. I become inattentive to the consistent goodness of God as revealed in people and creation around me.

So for these remaining days of Advent, I will try to awaken each morning and recommit my heart to "exulting in God" by seeing and welcoming with gratitude the numerous blessings that are mine. I will be grateful for the use of my body and mind, for the voices of those who care, for the hands and hearts that send letters of cheer, and for each moment that I breathe and have life. At evening I will again "exult in God" by calling to mind the joys my day has held.

 Giver of Life, I receive this day from you with a grateful heart.

Lent

The First Book of Revelation

Be holy, for I, the Lord, your God, am holy.

LEVITICUS
19:2

We had a joy-filled evening of song, dance, and storytelling at a retreat. The next day a participant remarked how refreshing it was to have a spiritual occurrence that was so much fun. She said she used to think an experience was holy only when we were thinking or speaking directly about God. She voiced a common misunderstanding—believing we have to be apart from life, rather than within life, in order to be communicating with divinity. To be holy "as God is holy" is to be in union with the One who created and loves us fully.

We have numerous opportunities to enter into this union. Shortly before his death, Pope John Paul II commented on experiencing God's goodness when he visited a place of beauty in the Italian Alps. He noted, "Creation is the first book of revelation." This comment reinforces the truth that the world, rather than separating us from the Holy One, can actually be a source of bringing us nearer to this divine presence.

Look into your life today. Where do you recognize the sacred? How is the goodness and beauty of God revealed in your own life, as well as in the world around you?

Ever-present God, may the eyes of my heart be clear enough to find you in every part of my life.

Compassion: "Your Pain in My Heart"

> But yours,
> O Lord,
> our God,
> are
> compassion
> and
> forgiveness!
>
> DANIEL
> 9:9

A sister in my community described compassion as "your pain in my heart." To carry another's hurt in our heart in order to help the other person bear his or her pain requires a generous amount of love and other-centeredness. For another's suffering to reach inside our heart, there must be a desire, an openness, and a willingness to let the pain reside there.

The "thought" of compassion is much more appealing than the actual deed. Although it is lauded in politics, medical centers, religious communities, large corporations, parishes, and educational staffs, compassion does not always get put into action.

"To offer the heart is not like offering a fingernail or a lock of hair we were ready to discard anyway; it is to offer the core, the most essential part of our being," writes author Sharon Salzberg. No wonder being compassionate is easier said than done.

Lent calls us back to living compassionately, not just praising the idea of it. To do this, we return to the compassion of God so beautifully mirrored in the teaching and ministry of Jesus. This compassion is more than an apt description; it is a way of life in which one truly embraces the suffering of another with genuine kindness, mercy, and unselfish care.

 Jesus, help me to carry the pain of others in my heart.

Surrendering with Peaceful Heart

Behold, we are going up to Jerusalem, and the Son of Man will be handed over...
MATTHEW
20:18

Jesus began his yielding process long before he reached the Garden of Olives and made his final bow of surrender on the cross. When he deliberately went up to Jerusalem, he already began the "handing over" process because he knew his enemies awaited him there. I was freshly inspired by this kind of profound surrender when a friend of mine died of ALS. She surrendered peacefully and welcomed death as a release into the arms of God, but not until she accepted being "handed over."

As with Jesus, this surrender did not come easily or instantly. About six months before Dorothy died, she explained to me in an anguished voice: "I am being handed over," meaning she was losing control of her bodily functions to ALS. She could no longer walk and had trouble swallowing and speaking. Truly, her disease was giving her over to death. This admission was the turning point for my friend, eventually leading her to accept her impending death. From then on, she entrusted herself totally to God, as Jesus did, and found peace of mind and heart in the final months before her life on earth ended. Her death reminds me that there is always more surrender required if I am to grow spiritually.

 Crucified One, grant me the wisdom to know what I am to surrender and the courage to do so.

21

Led by the Spirit

Jesus returned from the Jordan and was led by the Spirit into the desert...

LUKE 4:1

Jesus did not decide on his own to go into the desert. He was led there by the Spirit. Jesus would probably not have chosen to go there any more than any of us would choose to enter into an extended time of struggle. Yet in those challenging forty days Jesus experienced his inner strength and found a clear direction for his future ministry. Out of that empty and hostile sojourn, Jesus came forth "with the power of the Spirit" in him (Luke 4:14).

I can't imagine any of us liking our own deserts, the parts of our life we want to get rid of as fast as we can: disagreeable relationships, ongoing illness, unsatisfying work, troubling questions about religious beliefs, challenges to our ego and anything else that snatches us away from a contented life. We tend to think our deserts are bad places, but could it be the Spirit leads us there to help us know ourselves better? Could it be that our deserts are the very place where we meet our spiritual power, where our faith is strengthened, and the assurance is given that we can, as Jesus did, deliberately choose for good in the face of temptation and conflict?

 Spirit of God, I will enter the deserts of my life and trust that you are there.

"Signs to Help Me Change My Ways"

Just as Jonah became a sign to the Ninevites...

LUKE
11:30

Jonah was surprised when the people he preached to actually changed their ways and repented. Because of Jonah's urging and challenges, they re-turned their hearts toward God. Who are the people in our lives who are a sign to us? How do others draw us back to the heart of God when we need to be nudged in that direction?

I can think of so many who urge me to repent. Most of them give me a good boost to change my ways by the witness of their lives, more than by what they say. I am pulled away from my self-absorption when I observe the immense amount of time and care that parents give to their children. Compassionate people challenge my lack of caring and my failure to be there for others. Seriously ill persons, courageously facing their difficulties, draw me toward greater trust in God's unfailing strength. The poor who continue to give of the little they have remind me to be more generous with what I have. Those who forgive their betrayers and abusers urge me to do the same with those who have hurt me in any way. Each day I am given signs to help me change my ways. Like the Ninevites, I can do so.

 God of the prophets, thank you for all those messengers of yours who draw me back to you.

Sentinel Duty

> My soul waits for the Lord more than sentinels wait for the dawn.
>
> PSALM 130:6

Sentinels keep watch. Their duty is to guard a protected area and warn of anyone who might be approaching. Sentinels are to be constantly aware of the least noise and the slightest footstep. Imagine how difficult this is when sentinels have the night shift and must repeatedly fight the desire to doze off. The psalmist tells us we need this kind of alertness to recognize God's nearness.

Our times of silence, prayer, and solitude are our sentinel times. During this restorative period, we renew our ability to be aware of God's presence. We may grow tired of hearing about the importance of silence and the necessity of quiet time but this spiritual attentiveness is an absolute must. Our frenetic culture tempts us away from this spiritual alertness by offering us constant activity and unending noise. Be assured, our soul needs stillness. Like a sentinel guarding our mind and heart, stillness readies us to welcome God's presence during the busy parts of our day. When I remember the necessity of my "sentinel duty," I am not tempted to forgo my daily quiet time. When I struggle with my weariness or fall asleep during my "sentinel duty" I do not become discouraged. I begin again, knowing how vital this "time of watching" is.

 I will watch for you today, O God, and be alert to how you are with me.

Revitalizing Our Spirit

Life moves along quickly. We become immersed in our daily activities, distracted by the "have-to-dos" continually filling our minds and hearts, or lost in the dullness of daily routine. Our relationship with God frequently needs revitalization, much as the dry bones in Ezekiel's valley needed to be invigorated. During Lent, we address any spiritual fatigue we have by inquiring of ourselves: What in my spirit needs to return to life? What part requires new energy, renewed effort, some fresh oomph, in order to engage more fully with the process of my faith development and spiritual growth?

Has kindness or generosity withered into daily nagging and constant complaining? Has hope slumped into relentless discouragement? Has patience shriveled into harsh language? Has prayer dried up from neglect? Has peace of mind dissolved into compulsive anxiety? Now is the time to face whatever needs some renewed verve and vitality. Call it back to life with the same confidence that Ezekiel had in that valley of dry bones. Remember it was the movement of God's Spirit that came upon the dry bones and restored flesh to them. So, too, with what awaits enlivening in us.

 Spirit of God, energize the dead bones of my spiritual life. Restore what has grown weary in my relationship with you.

25

"A Thousand Roots Silently Drinking"

Along both banks of the river, fruit trees of every kind shall grow...
EZEKIEL 47:12

Imagine what a bountiful harvest there would be if scores of fruit trees lined both sides of a wide, flowing river. With their roots so near the water source, trees would be nourished and produce an abundant harvest. The variety of trees that grow along the river banks in the Ezekiel passage refer to this productivity and symbolize our spiritual plentitude when our roots are deep in the heart of God. We are the well-nourished trees. God is the Great River, the source of all grace and growth, the one who provides for our spirit's maturation. The fruits we bear are the virtues and qualities each Christian seeks to activate.

One of the ways the poet Maria Rainer Rilke pictured God was as a "thousand roots silently drinking." What a powerful image! Rilke also notes that these roots are in darkness, an image which assures us that even if we do not always sense God nourishing us, it is happening all the same, just as the hidden roots are nourishing the trees. If we trust and stay close to the stream of the Holy One, our roots of faith will be fed. God will provide us with the spiritual nourishment we need in order to bear abundant goodness in our life, even in the dry seasons.

 River of Life, thank you for your sustaining grace, nourishing my spirit at every moment.

Dropping the Heavy Stones of Hate

They picked up stones to throw at him.

JOHN 8:59

When Jesus responded to his challengers with, "Before Abraham came to be, I AM" (John 8:58), the people became angry with what he said and picked up stones to do him harm. "What a terrible thing to do," I think to myself, but then I remember the stones I've thrown when I've felt defensive, hostile, or insecure. Not physical stones, but verbal, mental, emotional ones, just as weighty and destructive as those that the people picked up as they threatened Jesus. Anyone who's been the object of harsh insults, snippy comments, and angry expletives knows that nonphysical stones achieve great hurt from the emotional bleeding they cause.

What kind of stones do people hurl at one another today? Certainly prejudice, self-righteousness, and cruel judgment are among the destructive missiles. But there are others: coldness, bitterness, jealousy, revenge, non-forgiveness, hatred. People throw these stones without fully realizing the damage they cause.

I suggest we each place a stone at our place of prayer for the coming week. Pick it up each day and hold it while we ponder any stone-tossing we've been tempted to do or have done. Pray for a change of heart.

 Dear God, help me to put my stones down when I want to hurl them at others. Help me to change my ways.

27

Oil Is a Symbol of God's Abundance

You anoint my head with oil; my cup overflows.

PSALM 23:5

Oil had a significant place in the worship of early Christian communities. Its usage gave special importance to their rituals, reminding them of the protective love of God. Because of oil's smooth quality and its facility to flow readily, it also symbolized the abundance of divine blessings. Today, blessed oils are used for administering special church sacraments as a sign of blessing and strengthening, but for little else. There are, of course, non-church uses of oil: parents rub it on their infant's skin to keep it soft, and massage therapists relax clients' tense muscles with warmed oil. Some indigenous people still use oil ritually to celebrate abundance, such as the Barabaig in Tanzania who anoint their successful hunters with butter.

Most modern churchgoers have lost the spiritual significance of anointing the body with oil. The spiritual question surrounding the use of oil for ritual in our era is this: Do we need a new symbol or can we revive the meaning of the ancient one? If not oil, what symbol might help us in our modern world to acknowledge the abundant banquet and lavish blessings of the Creator? Whatever symbol we use, let us often celebrate the wealth of God's goodness in our lives.

 Like oil softening the body, soften my heart, O God. I pray that my love will resemble your tender and abundant kindness.

The Divine Searcher Looks with Love

O searcher of heart and soul, O just God.

PSALM
7:10

There was a time when this psalm verse might have scared me. I would have been concerned about God roaming around in my inner world, finding things that were wrong with me. I would have tried to hide my weaknesses and imperfections by never mentioning them in my prayers, with the hope that God would not notice them. Now I feel quite differently. This verse actually encourages me. Not that I have gotten rid of all the things that keep me from being a loving person. What has changed is that I now believe that this Searcher of my heart looks with a gaze of kindness at my inner life. The Holy One believes in my inherent goodness and is aware of my desire to change what I can regarding my weaknesses and wrongdoings. I now believe that God is merciful and just, always for me and never against me.

I am also comforted by this verse because it reminds me of how near God is to me, so close that my soul can be found out. No part of my being is apart from the divine companion's presence. What a great gift. God is a strength and a grace, encouraging me to continue to turn toward love.

Companion

O Divine Searcher, I open my entire being to you, trusting in your mercy and kindheartedness.

29

Truth Forces Us from Comfort Zones

...the truth will set you free.

JOHN
8:32

"The truth may set you free," said one theologian, "but it may make a lot of other people extremely annoyed." Truth brings personal freedom, but it can also bring about harsh judgments. Sometimes when a person grows into a new attitude or behavior, other people become uncomfortable with the results. They frown on the new freedom because it doesn't meet their expectations of how they've known that person. They are often unable to accept the unsettling changes that tend to accompany new behavior.

There is a true story of a man who cared twenty years for his disabled wife. During all this time, he was a tremendously loving and attentive spouse. Several years after his wife died, he remarried. One night he and his new wife were at a social gathering with old friends. During the evening he began dancing and singing. Several who had known him as a quiet, self-contained man whispered that he shouldn't be "doing things like that." His new behavior disrupted their comfort zone. In their mind, he was supposed to be calm and reserved as he had always been. They refused to accept his newly found joy and inner freedom after his long years as a dedicated caregiver.

Help me respect newly found truths in myself and in others, God, as we continue to grow into the persons you desire us to be.

30

Protection for Our Hearts

For he has strengthened the bars of your gates...

PSALM
147:13

Psalm 147 praises God for being a guardian of the people, one who strengthens the gates leading into Jerusalem. These gates were a necessary protection for those who lived within the city. These barriers needed to be strong so enemies could not get inside to harm the occupants. Like the city in this psalm, our hearts need protection. The enemies that threaten to hurt our inner realm of integrity are many. The gates of our heart need to be strong so the love that God has placed there will not be harmed or destroyed.

Strong bars on our heart are required so nothing can get in to steal or harm our ability to love well. We need protection against resentments and hurts that try to leap through and destroy our desire to forgive. Selfishness and lack of gratitude rust and weaken the inner gates. Our heart needs protection to resist the voice of the culture telling us to stake our happiness solely on material things. Daily prayer and vigilant attention are the inner gates that help keep these and other enemies from breaking through and harming our spiritual well-being.

 Protect my heart from what takes me away from you, Beloved Companion. Grant me wisdom to choose wisely, to know when to bar my heart and when to keep it wide open.

31

Life-Giving Water

> Wherever the river flows, every sort of living creature that can multiply shall live...
>
> EZEKIEL 47:9

In the bible water is usually a symbol of a significant blessing. This Scripture reading speaks about the life-giving aspect of water. God offers this significant image to Ezekiel as a sign of hope. The river that flows is the river of life. The prophet has not had an easy life. He has come through tough times but now he is assured by the Holy One that good things will happen. Fruitfulness will come forth from Ezekiel's dedicated efforts on God's behalf.

This Scripture passage invites us to trust that new life can follow death, that happiness can rise up out of sadness, that peace of mind and heart can evolve after a painful experience. Whatever has burdened and weighed heavily on our heart can eventually be set aside. The river of divine care runs without end. We can all participate and benefit from it.

Take time today to notice water and its effects. As you wash your hands, take a drink, do the dishes, enjoy a shower, water a plant, wash clothes, pay attention to what water does. Pray a prayer of trust to the God of life who breathes newness into what seems lifeless, to the one who restores what has grown dull in our inner world.

 Water of Life, I am grateful for the countless ways you restore and renew my relationship with you.

Praise God

How can you believe, when you accept praise from one another and do not seek the praise that comes from the only God?

JOHN 5:44

I grew up in a family where adults believed the less you praised someone the better, lest that person become too proud. But praise is actually an essential component of positive human development. We all need it. True praise, not false flattery, helps us believe in and accept the talents and virtuous qualities God has bestowed on us. How else would the Holy One praise us except by speaking through the sincere comments coming from others? Accepting praise in a spiritually healthy way, however, depends on how we receive those kind words. "Thank you" is the best response to genuine praise, with the humble understanding that who we are is due to the Giver of all gifts. The "praise underneath the praise" always belongs to God.

Someone asked me not long ago how I handle the positive responses I receive about my writing and retreats. I explained that I try to accept these accolades graciously, but then I let the praise wash off of me. If I hang on to it, I quickly forget it is God who works through me. True praise comes from God, and true praise is due back to God for what has been given.

 I praise you, Giver of Gifts, for the positive attributes you have provided me. May I use these gifts humbly in service of others.

33

Living Generously and Lovingly

For we are his handiwork, created in Christ Jesus for the good works that God has prepared in advance, that we should live in them.

EPHESIANS 2:10

We come from the hand of God, created with all we need to live in a loving manner. Who of us comprehends this amazing reality? Do we believe we are the handiwork of the Creator? Many find it difficult to grasp this reality. Some persons are quick to discount aspects of their personalities and actions even though they reflect God's goodness. These "handiworks" seem way too common, too ordinary. The self-talk might go like this: "There's not much about the way I live that's noteworthy. I see other people who seem better than I am. They are much holier than I am. I wish I could be like him or her."

The seemingly insignificant aspects of our honorable actions are a reflection of the way God created us. As we listen to the hurt of another, overlook the impatience or irritability of a colleague, forgive a friend who disappointed us, take time to do a good deed, or refuse to add to gossip, we are expressing the truth of being God's handiwork. During Lent, let us remember that we have been created with the essential ingredients for living in a generously loving and caring way. Let us believe it!

 May I live this day in fuller awareness of being your handiwork, O God.

Turning My Whole Self to God

They turned their backs, not their faces, to me... they have stiffened their necks.

JEREMIAH
7:24, 26

The prophet Jeremiah proclaims God's message of renewal through verbal illustrations of the human body. These metaphors aptly describe how closed down and stubborn the people are. They turn their backs and move in the opposite direction. They will not face God. They stiffen their necks, refusing to live as God longs for them to live.

How easy it is to shut the other out, to close down, to move away from or refuse to look at someone. Silence can be used as a response to avoid communication. Stubbornness keeps needed communication from taking place. This church season is the time to turn our whole self toward God. It is the season of softening our stiff necks and bending our pride. It is the time to turn toward, rather than away from, those who test our love, to humbly accept the challenge of living as the Holy One desires us to live. Lent encourages us to break our silence, to speak with those whom we have avoided or refused to acknowledge, and to extend our forgiveness to those who have hurt us. Now is the time to hear the cry of Jeremiah and heed the voice of our Beloved: "Turn around and come back to me. I am waiting for your return."

 Turn my heart toward love, God, turn my heart.

Do I Really Want to Be Healthy?

Do you want to be well?

JOHN
5:6

Jesus asked a simple question of the man who had been ill for 38 years: "Do you want to be well?" Knowing the man's situation, one might think "Of course he does. Why bother to ask?" But the question is important, because sometimes people would rather be sick than be well. A woman once told me she had spent most of her life being sick, wishing she could die because she felt she was of little worth. With good counseling and spiritual guidance she finally began to change her view of herself and her illnesses lessened.

Sometimes the desire to be sick may come from a simple thing like wanting a day off from work, or trying to get some extra attention from others, or being too lazy or too busy to exercise, eat well and get enough sleep. Of course, not every person with extended illness desires to be sick but the question Jesus asks is a vital one for us to ponder. Do we truly want to be healthy in body, mind, and spirit? If so, then we must do our part to help that to happen. Now is the time to review how we treat our body, to notice what we allow to dwell in our mind and heart, and to review how much care we give to our relationship with God.

 Divine Companion, teach me how to be healthy in body, mind and spirit.

A Time to Evaluate Our Responses

I have shown you many good works from my Father. For which of these are you trying to stone me?

JOHN 10:32

The people around Jesus threatened to harm him because they did not like what he was saying. They did not know what to make of him because of his surprising healings and challenging messages. His teachings and actions carried the message of kindness and compassion. Yet, some people were threatened by his good works and beliefs because taking Jesus' teachings to heart meant they would have to change their ways. Instead, they responded with fear and anger, deciding to stone Jesus as a means of punishment.

Stoning may not be a common method for punishing someone in our culture, but people still react at times with violence when they feel threatened. Some of these responses include racial slurs, negative judgments, harsh condemnation, silencing, social shaming, and verbal abuse. Lent is a time when we can be more attentive to how we respond to those who are different from us. We can listen for any prejudice, animosity, or hatred that our thoughts or words might hold when we think of undocumented immigrants, homosexuals, or other people who often receive hateful rejection and verbal antipathy.

 Divine Creator, you have brought each of us into this world as unique human beings. Help me to respect the diversity of others and to not fear our differences.

37

How Many Prisoners Am I Holding?

Saying to the prisoners: Come out!

ISAIAH 49:9

When something is held captive in us, it is much like a person in prison. This creates a lack of freedom, holds us back, closes us off. I find there's always something more that needs to be freed in me. Just when I think I've let the last prisoner out of my inner cell, I locate another one that needs to be released. Most recently, I discovered I was holding "acceptance of others" in my prison.

A new man started working at my local post office. He was obese, huffing and puffing at his counter, and rude to everyone. I didn't like him and found myself hoping each time that I'd be waited on by someone else. One day a little voice in me said, "Let me out!" I looked at the man I disliked and asked God to help me be kind to him. I made a deliberate effort to be cheerful. This went on for several weeks. One day when I stood at the counter I thought, "He's cleaned up a bit, lost some weight, and is much more friendly." But then as I walked out I thought, "Did he change or did I?" At that moment "acceptance of others" walked out of my inner prison.

 Help me to recognize what I hold captive in my heart, O God, and to release the prisoners I have put behind the bars of my unloving.

God Is Like the Spring Rain

[God] will come to us like the rain, like spring rain that waters the earth.

HOSEA 6:3

In the northern hemisphere of our planet, it is springtime during Lent. How I enjoy the spring rains, especially the soft and steady ones. The welcome showers wash old residue away. The rains heal the land by softening and opening up the tightly wintered soil, enabling it to become more porous and receptive. The prophet Hosea aptly describes God's presence among us as this kind of spring rain. Hosea felt strongly that God's coming could bring hope and healing.

I am reminded of an old song by the Medical Missionary Sisters: "I saw raindrops on my window, joy is like the rain." Yes, God has been like a spring rain in my life, especially when I was the most wintered and hard-hearted. Healing has come in the form of understanding and compassionate persons who forgave me for my faults and failings, who listened to my resolute complaints about life situations without chiding me for my self pity and my inability to move on from hurt, who softened my heart by simply loving me. Yes, God is like the spring rain, cleansing and restorative, often coming through people who reflect this beautiful and healing aspect of divinity.

Thank you, God, for the countless times you have come into my life like a spring rain, and for the persons who helped to heal and renew my inner landscape.

Faith Isn't About Feeling Good

They forgot the God who had saved them, who had done great deeds in Egypt...

PSALM
106:21

The Israelites were frustrated in the desert. The people were tired of being homeless, of wandering and feeling lost. They detested their daily sustenance and lacked confidence in their leaders. Actually, the Israelites didn't appear to feel good about much of anything that was going on in their wilderness journey. They did not want to put up with the process any longer, so they built a golden calf, a false god they thought would be able to help them more than the God of Moses.

I've been in that desert where obstacles predominated. I've been there on days when everything goes wrong. Such occasions tempt me away from trust in God at the very time when I actually need to lean more strongly on the Beloved. I, too, have wanted a golden calf of false securities to help me feel good, to free me from annoyances and release me from irritations. But faith is not about feeling good and having complete security. Faith is about trusting God in both the good and the not-so-good times. When life becomes difficult, rather than building a golden calf of anxiety, worry, or resentment, I need to wait with patient faith and enduring hope, trusting the One who never leaves me alone in my time of troubles.

 When life is difficult, keep my heart focused on your abiding presence, O God.

In Receiving, We Give

Mary took a liter of costly perfumed oil...and anointed the feet of Jesus...
JOHN
12:3

What was it like for Jesus to have Mary anoint his feet? From all indications, he seems to have appreciated what she did for him. Without a word of protest, he receives the loving gesture and full attention of Mary. Furthermore, he tells the apostles to "leave her alone" when they are bothered by the expensive perfume she uses for the anointing and complain to him about it.

This is another good message from the gospel for those of us who would prefer to be in charge, who want to do for others rather than be the one to receive. I myself have had to discover the value in being the receiver and not always the giver. I have had to learn that when I allow someone else to do a kindness for me, my receptivity becomes a gift for them. I usually gain a sense of satisfaction and self-worth when I help others in any kind of gracious or loving way. So if I balk at or refuse to receive another's kindness, I am, in a sense, denying them the pleasure they could have by tending to my needs.

 Anointed One, when I want to give rather than receive, grant me the gift of humble receptivity so that I can graciously accept what is offered to me.

The Suffering of the Persecuted

[Then] they tried again to arrest him; but he escaped from their power.

JOHN
10:39

Reading Caryll Houselander's books long ago (especially *This War is the Passion* and *The Way of the Cross*) taught me a profound truth: The suffering Christ lives on in our humanity. Houselander helped me see that we continue to meet the Crucified One in the pain-filled lives of those around us and in our larger world. She writes, "...because (Christ's) life continues in each one of us, there is nothing that any of us can suffer which is not the passion he suffered." All suffering people bear a resemblance to the anguished Jesus, but especially those who face cruel opposition and the threat of violence from others.

We do not have to look far today to see Christ suffering in the persecuted. The Crucified One is reflected in each person who endures suffering at the hands of another. Many people struggle to escape the power of those who try to hurt them: children in war-torn countries, political prisoners condemned for their fight on behalf of justice, women caught in sexual exploitation, people controlled by drug- and warlords, the mentally ill enduring society's rejection, refugees refused a welcome in foreign lands, and the elderly in nursing homes who experience abuse and neglect.

Crucified One, I will pause today and unite my heart with those whose pain resembles that of yours on the cross.

The High Price of Selling Out

What are you willing to give me if I hand him over to you?

MATTHEW 26:15

When we barter away our goodness and our integrity, we pay a price for it. Judas asked how many coins he would receive for handing Jesus over to his enemies. When we give ourselves over to that which is detrimental for us, it depletes us of something much more valuable than money. This action diminishes our self worth and lessens our personal integrity.

I still remember in eighth grade a time when I dishonestly won a prize for selling magazines. No one knew I had lied except myself. In a moment of greed and desire for recognition, I handed over what I valued greatly: my honesty and some of my self-esteem. I lost it by doing something that went against my better judgment. This was a significant lesson for me in my youth. It comes back to me time and again when I am tempted to be less than I know I am or can be. Whether it's speaking ill of others, exaggerating or bending the truth, being haughty or selfish, or whatever tempts me to sell my self for something less, I remember there is a price to be paid for it.

 Giver of Integrity, keep me aware of my self worth when I want to sell my goodness or barter my integrity for the sake of some momentary satisfaction.

Easter
to
Pentecost

A Spirituality of Gladness

All you peoples, clap your hands, shout to God with cries of gladness.

PSALM
47:2

Easter is a season of joy. Why is it that problems, troubles, and worries usually get center stage in the spiritual life? Why is joy a neglected part of prayer? Most of us surely do enough complaining and beseeching of God when things don't go our way. How can we balance our requests and wants with thanksgiving and joy? One way I've found to nurture a spirituality of gladness is by remembrance. Each day before closing my eyes for sleep, I look back over the day that is ending. No matter how troublesome the day has been, I recover my joy by asking: "What is one thing in this day for which I can be glad?"

There is always something that can bring joy. Maybe I managed to get through the day without any physical or emotional discomfort. Maybe it was a kind word, a comforting thought, a little hug, or an unexpected bird winging by. Sometimes I discover in remembrance that I missed the day's happy moments because I was overly focused on just one thing that didn't go as I planned or because someone did not meet my expectations.

I hope that I never let a day go by without glimpsing a touch of joy in it and crying out to God with gladness.

 Risen Christ, may the joyfulness of this Easter season find a home in my heart.

Sharing My Relationship with God

After their release they went back to their own people and reported what the chief priests and elders had told them.

ACTS
4:23

Why are some of us reluctant to bring our personal relationship with God into conversation? Why is it much easier to talk about external events rather than internal ones? Not long ago, five of my religious community members and I had a profoundly enriching experience as we shared who God is for us now. I felt strengthened and renewed by hearing their hopes, struggles, and desires. Afterward, I thought about how our deep, honest sharing was an exception rather than a regular occurrence.

Perhaps we do not talk at a deeper level because our relationship with the Holy One is so intimate. Our reluctance may also be due to a sense of inadequacy or a concern that our experience of God won't sound "good enough" if we are truly honest about the times when we feel empty, questioning, unsure, confused, or doubtful about this relationship. Such sharing requires a willingness to be open and honest. While this may be difficult to do, it is these vulnerable moments that strengthen our bond with one another. Like the early Christian community after Easter, this deeper sharing encourages us to draw near to God. Today, let's risk talking with someone close to us about our relationship with God.

 Dear God, release in me whatever prevents my being willing and able to talk about my relationship with you.

48

Trusting in God's Hidden Presence

The wind blows where it wills... but you do not know where it comes from or where it goes.

JOHN
3:8

This passage reminds me of a woman who sent an old black-and-white photograph to a photofinishing company. In the photo, a man was seated behind a cow. All that was visible of him were his feet and his legs. Her accompanying note read: "This is the only photo I have of my great-grandfather. Please remove the cow so I can see what he looks like."

Faith is about trusting without seeing the whole picture. As much as we yearn to know and understand fully we can only see a small part of who God is and why our life unfolds as it does. We comprehend just a tiny portion of the meaning of events and circumstances that affect us. No matter how much we pray and study, we cannot fully explain the divine mystery that lies within and beyond us. All that is required is that we daily place our hand in the Holy One's with confidence and walk lovingly in life. We do not need all the answers, only to trust and believe that the Mysterious One is as near to us as the slightest breeze or the strongest wind. Let us renew our faith in this hidden presence today.

 Spirit of God, grant that I may be at peace with that which I do not understand or comprehend. I place my trust in your constant presence.

49

An Extension of Our Faith

> After [Lydia] and her household had been baptized, she offered us an invitation, "...come and stay at my home," and she prevailed on us.
>
> ACTS
> 16:15

My parents were known for their hospitality. Often a salesman would show up at the family farm shortly before the noon meal. Word got around of my mother's delicious cooking and my father's generous invitations to "stay for lunch." As a child, I never questioned having a stranger at our table. I thought every family extended this kind of welcome. Such hospitality is reflected in Lydia's story. She was thrilled with her newly found faith, so much so that she readily invited strangers to stay with her.

Lydia could have gone home and basked in the wonder of what she had experienced in her baptism. Instead, she opened her life and her home, thinking of others as she reached out to them. Her act of kindness models Christian faith. Our personal relationship with God needs to be vital and primary in our lives as it was in Lydia's. This relationship takes us outward to extend love and kindness to others. Lydia never hugged her faith to herself. Neither should we. Let us ask ourselves today: What has my faith given to me? How am I sharing it?

 May my faith move me toward action. May my relationship with you, God, be seen in how I respond to others.

50

Patience in the Face of Death's Mystery

I have much more to tell you, but you cannot bear it now.

JOHN 16:12

Jesus knew the disciples were not ready to know everything about his teachings and, thus, he did not tell them everything at once. The disciples had to be satisfied with the unknown, to be patient with what would unfold for them when their ability to understand was more mature. The same is true for us. I have found this reality difficult when facing the heart of mystery, especially when I have tried to figure out what lies on the other side of this life.

Recently, I experienced the death of four significant people in my life. When each one of them died, I wanted to know where they were and how they were. In this Easter season, I am reminded that it all comes down to faith. As with the disciples, I, too, "cannot bear it now." The vital thing is to believe and trust that my loved ones are in the embrace of an all-welcoming God. When my own time of death comes, I will know what eternity is. For now, I do not need to have it figured out or to have my questions answered. I only wish to be humbly patient as I wait for the unfolding of this great mystery.

 God of Life, teach me how to let my mind and heart be at rest with what I am not yet able to fully understand.

Marital Union Comes with a Price

...a man shall leave his father and mother [and be joined to his wife], and the two shall become one flesh.

MARK
10:7–8

When Jesus described marriage as "becoming one flesh," he was speaking of more than sexual union. He was emphasizing the profound oneness and unity of relationship that evolves for married couples who truly give themselves to their vowed commitment. When I reflect on the people I know who have been happily married for many years, I realize that their harmony of mind, heart, and body comes with a price. Happy and faithful marriages do not "just happen." Each time they consider the other person's needs and listen to his or her hopes and desires, they open the way toward greater oneness. Each time they forgive after a fight, each time they let go of their aggravating patterns of behavior, each time they stop insisting their way is the only way, they are shaping a bond that reflects the beauty of God's love.

 Jesus, you valued marriage and saw the beauty this union could have if it was lived with care and loving consideration for one another. May your love especially imbue all married couples who have forgotten the treasure of oneness and have neglected thoughtful, loving gestures of kindness toward each other. Wake them up and encourage them to renew their relationship with one another and with you.

Don't Let Anyone Steal Your Joy

There was great joy in that city.
ACTS 8:8

When Philip went to Samaria, he healed the wounded ones the crowd brought to him. The people were elated at what took place. Joy comes in varied forms and it is always a valuable gift. With the current turmoil of the world, it is difficult to keep a spirit of joy in one's heart. I recall hearing a comment some time ago that helps keep my joy alive: "Beware of those who try to steal your joy from you." Usually people do not steal our happiness deliberately. We allow them to take it from us. I can wake up alive and grateful for the beauty and goodness of life. Then, someone enters my day crabby and disgruntled. If I'm not careful to guard my joy, I am soon feeling grumpy, too.

Similarly, I might go to a church service eager to be renewed. Then I allow the poorly prepared liturgy to dull my spirit instead of reaching deeper into my heart to where true contentment resides. How difficult to retain my inner harmony and not allow it to be overcome by the behavior and attitudes of others.

Joy is a precious gift from God. Treasure it and protect it as best you can.

 Source of all joy, remind me often that you have given the kind of contentment and peace that no one and no thing can ever take from me.

"God Experiences"

They were startled and terrified and thought that they were seeing a ghost.

LUKE
24:37

Some time ago I met two persons, at separate events, who had unusual spiritual experiences. One woman at a retreat described a vision of Jesus she had many years ago. Another told of a childhood moment when she saw her guardian angel. Neither one expected these encounters to take place but each person valued their experience and allowed it to influence their faith. These extraordinary events remind me of how terrified the disciples were when they met the Risen Christ. The encounter was totally unexpected, and greatly dismayed them, but later it had a significant impact on their faith.

When "God experiences" don't fit our expectations, it is very easy to dismiss or try to rationalize them out of existence. Yet, they do happen to some people, most of whom say nothing for fear of being ridiculed or considered delusional. Most of us will not have this type of intense divine encounter. If we stop to consider the possibility, though, we do have daily events that surprise us with the Risen Christ's presence. Touches of surprising beauty, unexpected generosity, and unanticipated caring enter our lives on a regular basis. These events might not be exceptional visionary experiences, but they do bring with them a sense of wonder at how the Risen One enters our life and greets us.

 Keep me open and aware of how you enter my life, Risen Christ.

Come, Holy Spirit!

For the one whom God sent… does not ration his gift of the Spirit.

JOHN
3:34

The gifts of the Spirit of God are available to anyone who asks and is ready to receive them. As a way of encouraging you to welcome these spiritual gifts, I share with you this prayer:

Come, Holy Spirit, help me replace the busyness of my life with a simpler lifestyle, so I will focus on the essential things in life and allow time for others. Nourish my ability to understand and appreciate myself. Keep me from being too self-oriented and unmindful of others' needs.

Fill me with trust in your consoling presence. Calm me when I am anxious and troubled. Help me to have the courage to empty myself of anything that does not contribute to the transformation of this world.

Continue to create a deep hunger for you within me. Feed me with "the finest wheat" of your joy, peace, and love. Replenish my weary spirit with an enthusiasm and energy that comes from surrendering my life to you.

Be my wisdom as I search for meaning in a world fraught with pain, suffering, hostility, and division.

Keep me hungry for you, Source of Life, so that I will always ache and yearn for you.

Stop Muttering, Start Listening!

Were not our hearts burning [within us] while he spoke to us on the way and opened the Scriptures to us?

LUKE
24:32

The image of the two disciples encountering Jesus as they walked toward Emmaus has always been inspiring for me. When I consider what they must have felt like, I can relate to their low morale. In my relationship with Jesus, I, too, am on the road of life where I meet the Risen One. I also have my moments when I feel discouraged and dismayed. Like the disciples, I have the possibility of a Christ-encounter that can change my heart and restore peace to my disconsolate self.

My problem is that I become engrossed and preoccupied with my mutterings, ramblings, and concerns and forget to notice God's loving presence. I whine and complain about "how life should be" and how my days contain way too much in them. After I get stuck in grumblings, it eventually occurs to me to turn to my Friend who's always been there. I stop muttering and start listening. Soon after I do this, something turns around inside of me. Call it peace, surrender, or whatever you will. All I know is that this is probably the closest I come to experiencing how the disciples' hearts ignited with love when they realized who was with them.

 When I lose my awareness of you, Risen Christ, lighten up my heart and bring me home to you again.

56

God's Grace Moves through Us

...why do you look so intently at us as if we had made him walk by our own power or piety?

ACTS
3:12

When the man crippled from birth was healed, Peter spoke convincingly to the crowd that gathered. He reminded them that the man's healing was due to the grace of God moving through the disciples, rather than by their own holiness or personal power. The fact that Peter acknowledged this is remarkable. What a transformation. This is the same man who once boldly set out to walk on the water, thinking he could manage it by himself. That is, of course, until he began to sink and cried out to Jesus to catch his hand and hold him up. Peter learned he needed divine strength and grace to help him in whatever he was doing. He came to realize that he could not do it all alone.

So, too, with us. Inner change and positive experiences do not happen by our single-handed efforts. The Holy Spirit moving through us enables these things to occur. We have only to open our minds and hearts, to receive what is available, to acknowledge the gifts God has given us, and allow the Spirit to activate those gifts. In doing so, we trust that divine grace will move through us to create positive change for ourselves and others.

 Spirit of God, thank you for empowering me each moment of my life.

Recognizing a Companion of Jesus

...they recognized them as the companions of Jesus.

ACTS
4:13

People were amazed at the ability of Peter and John to heal the sick and proclaim the message of Jesus. They knew these two men to be uneducated and ordinary and did not consider them exceptional enough to be instruments of God.

Throughout my life, I've been influenced by people who are "companions of Jesus." They are not out of the ordinary, yet their presence touches my heart and inspires me to want to be like them. One such person was an alcoholic priest who humbly admitted his addiction, went through a recovery program, and then, spent the rest of his life helping others with their addictions. Another was a blind woman who accepted her disability and moved beyond it to continually reach out quietly and lovingly to anyone in need.

Another person who influenced my faith was a leader in my religious community. She believed in my ability to give retreats and encouraged me to do so at a time when I felt incapable of trying to attempt that kind of ministry.

These persons and numerous others have taught me that to be a companion of Jesus does not take extraordinary talent and skill. It only needs someone who tries to embody the kind of love that was a part of all Jesus said and did.

 Thank you for those persons who have taught me what it means to be your companion, Jesus.

Festivals

Learning True Humility

FEBRUARY 22 • CHAIR OF ST. PETER, APOSTLE

Do not lord it over those assigned to you...
1 PETER
5:3

Is this the same Peter, the one who brashly told Jesus he would follow him anywhere but later denied him three times? Is this the same apostle who proudly leapt forward to walk across the water like Jesus did and is now advising, "Don't lord it over others"? Yes, this is the one and same Peter. Only now, he is different.

Humbled by his weakness and failure, Peter has seen his shadow side, his tendency toward pride and boasting. Through this, Peter discovered the wisdom of not lording it over others. Peter also learned true humility from Jesus as he watched him humbly move with ease among the downtrodden and wash the disciples' feet. After failing to acknowledge the message of his teacher, Peter finally got it. That is what lends weight to his advice.

Although Peter addressed his counsel to church leaders, everyone can take his words to heart. Many are the temptations to lord it over others by thinking we are better, know more than they do, or are morally superior. The more we come to know our own faults and acknowledge our failures, the less likely we are to lord it over anyone. Then we realize that while we may be different from someone else, we are not better than he or she is.

 Great Teacher, I desire to learn true humility and to live it well.

Silence Helps Us to Listen

MARCH 25 • FEAST OF THE ANNUNCIATION

May it be done to me according to your word.

LUKE
1:38

The power of the Annunciation is certainly contained in Mary's "yes" to God. Because she listened attentively to her inner life, Mary heard the invitation to be the mother of Jesus. To listen with awareness is almost impossible without eliminating some of the external and internal noise that consistently spills in on us. When we are continually crowded with noise, we miss hearing what is vital for our spiritual growth. Our external world is surely more noisy than Mary's, but our inner world might not be all that different from hers. When we are being asked by God to stretch, to deepen, to become more of our true self, many of us struggle with the same questions she did. As humans we each have intruding thoughts and emotions: "I'm not good enough. I don't know how. What will become of me? What will others think? Is this for real? How can I trust this is the will of God?"

Mary stilled her interruptive thoughts and emotions, but only after she paid attention to them. She was then able to trust God with the silent emptiness that filled her. We, too, have the grace to say "yes" to God if we will be silent enough to listen. In order to do this, we need to acknowledge and tend to our inner noise.

 Mary, Mother of Jesus, I turn to you and find confidence that I, too, can listen to the voice of God.

Misjudging Others

MAY 1 • ST. JOSEPH THE WORKER

Is he not the carpenter's son?
MATTHEW
13:55

Those who observed Jesus as he preached and healed questioned how he could have such wisdom and skills when he was "only the carpenter's son." Joseph's work seemed too common to have influenced someone as remarkable as Jesus. My initial response to their disbelief is: "How foolish of them to have judged Joseph that way."

Yet I sometimes find myself doing the same thing. I'm in awe of someone winning a Nobel Peace prize but completely inattentive to a woman cleaning my hotel room. I marvel at someone who can climb Mt. Everest but fail to notice the remarkable efforts of a single parent working diligently to raise her children. Each person has value and worth, but I too easily allow myself to evaluate people by considering certain activities as more worthy than others.

This feast day invites me to reflect on my approach to others. Do I ignore certain people because their work seems menial or insignificant? Can I be more respectful of everyone who works, regardless of the nature of their efforts? Little do I know which person, famous or unknown, is doing their work in a way that transforms their heart, thus bringing more love and goodness into our world.

 St. Joseph, pray for me that I will respect each person's worth and work, no matter how ordinary or exceptional it seems to be.

The Riches in the Heart of Christ

JUNE 23 • SACRED HEART OF JESUS

To me, the very least of all the holy ones, this grace was given, to preach to the Gentiles the inscrutable riches of Christ...

EPHESIANS 3:8

Sometimes we meet that rare person who's overflowing with goodness. The quality of his or her being has such genuine love that we almost can't believe this love to be true. Yet, we know it is because we have been the recipient of that authentic kindness. When we meet these loving persons, we long to be in their presence. How much more so with the person of Christ.

Can we ever fully realize how immense the love of Christ is for us? I think not. As we partake of his unconditional goodness, we can express our appreciation for what his love offers us through our daily prayer. In the heart of Christ we find complete mercy and total forgiveness, immense depths of compassion for our greatest sorrow and smallest ache, careful guidance for our spiritual path, understanding for our confusions, patience with our questions, unwavering peace for our tense and anxious spirits, and joy-filled beauty to draw us into consolation and assurance of God's love. These gifts and much more await us as the inscrutable riches of Christ are poured into our hearts.

 Heart of Christ, what a treasure I have in the riches of your unconditional love. May my heart resound with your goodness.

64

Focusing Only on "Effectiveness"

JUNE 24 • NATIVITY OF ST. JOHN THE BAPTIST

**I thought
I had
toiled in
vain...**
ISAIAH
49:4

We cannot always see the positive effects of our good efforts. In prison, John the Baptist wondered if his preaching had been worth it, if what he had done to support Jesus had made a difference. What John believed and taught appeared to be of no account. As he sat in the dungeon of his discouragement, John was considering the possibility that his life was a failure. He was so distraught he even sent his disciples to ask Jesus about this concern. I dare say most of us have raised a similar question about our own efforts at one time or another, no matter what our profession or way of life.

In prison, John would not have believed that one day he would be proclaimed a saint and revered for his dedicated life. When John was eventually beheaded, he did not know that he would be forever remembered in Scripture for his dedication and service as a precursor of Jesus.

When we place too much emphasis on results and effectiveness, we can misjudge our life and get caught in erroneous beliefs and self-doubts about our work. We will never fully know in this life the complete impact of the good we have done. It is enough to know that we have given our best.

 May my intentions be noble and my actions commendable, God. May I not doubt the value of their worth.

A Surprising Closeness

AUGUST 6 • TRANSFIGURATION OF JESUS

> And he was transfigured before them, and his clothes became dazzling white...
>
> MARK
> 9:2-3

In both of today's Scripture readings, the color white is used. The Ancient One in Daniel has hair "white as wool" and in Mark's Gospel, Jesus' clothes are "dazzling white." This color connotes transcendence, innocence, and sacredness. In many religions and in literature white symbolizes death to an old life and birth to a new, hope-filled one.

The disciples who witnessed Jesus in his glory could never be the same after that moment. This powerful experience birthed them into a more intimate and deeper relationship with their Teacher than they had ever known. The contemplative moment marked their inner selves forever. The same is true for us in our transfiguring moments, those times when we know from a simple, yet profound, experience that God is with us in a surprising closeness previously unimagined. This sense of divine presence might be in the brief space of receiving Eucharist, the surprise of hearing someone express their love for us, or any experience that catches us off guard when it draws us into a keener sense of God's being with us. When these moments take place, they usually intensify our relationship and renew our desire to be in union with the Holy One.

 Surprise me today, God, with the wonder of your presence. My heart is open and ready to respond.

Holiness Is More Than Showiness

NOVEMBER 1 • ALL SAINTS DAY

They stood before the throne and before the Lamb, wearing white robes and holding palm branches in their hands.
REVELATION
7:9

The image of holy people in white robes holding palm branches is serene and comforting, but becoming a saint involves a messy, human process, not a neat and tidy one as many envision it to be. Canonized saints made mistakes, failed, sinned, experienced discouragement and depression, and struggled with relationships—just like we all do. What made them saints was not their white robes or their unblemished lives, but their daily attempt to grow in virtue and goodness by relying on God's grace to help them to grow. They did not give up on their intention to be at one with the divine heart and they never quit trying to live in a manner that echoed this eternal goodness.

A holy life regularly reflects the goodness of God in myriad ways. It is made up not of showy deeds, but of a lifelong series of quiet acts of generous kindness that sustain and renew others. A saint's life contains little gestures of love that bring comfort and joy. Regular practice of this way of life prepares saints-in-the-making for the time when an immense deed of love might be required and expected of them.

 Eternal Love, I bring you my desire to be a person of unbounded love. With your grace I can be a reflection of your amazing goodness.

Remembering the Unfinished Souls

NOVEMBER 2 • ALL SOULS DAY

> Hear,
> O Lord,
> the sound
> of my call;
> have pity
> on me, and
> answer
> me.
>
> PSALM
> 27:7

There are souls who depart this life unfinished and unprepared for the next. They may have been persons who died performing acts of violent hatred and greed, or any human being who still had more living to do. The Church teaches that these souls need to continue their process of becoming the true self that God longs for them to be. These souls we call to mind and pray for on All Souls Day. We unite compassionately with those who have gone before us, praying that their life beyond this one is blessed with everlasting peace and complete union with God. We bring them to the Holy One in our prayer as we cry out for mercy and for their deliverance from an unfinished state of transformation.

All Souls Day is also a call to each of us to look and see whether we are being the kind of person God yearns for us to be. This day is a sobering time to remember that we, too, will one day leave this life and travel on to the next. All Souls Day invites us to look around at the closest people in our lives and see if we have loved them well enough.

 I bring all souls who have died and are in need of a completed transformation to you, Compassionate One. Touch them with your mercy and gather them to your heart.

Ordinary Time

Expanding the Circle of Gratitude

> Give thanks to the Lord... proclaim all his wondrous deeds.
>
> PSALM 105:1, 2

There are people unable to find much for which to be grateful: parents who cannot provide the essentials for their family, homeless persons seeking shelter each night, millions of AIDS orphans without anyone to care for them, wounded war victims lacking medical attention, lonely people in care centers, abused women, and so on.

How easy for someone like me to encourage others to follow Psalm 105's advice to give thanks. Like other Church leaders and members, I often forget what a rich life I have in comparison to others. It is easy for me to be filled with gratitude for what I have.

Perhaps those of us whose life bears plenitude can best express our thankfulness by assisting those whose life has little for which to be grateful. We can help widows find comfort when they are suddenly all alone. We can welcome the addicted without judgment and guide them into recovery programs, provide information and aid for those who are hungry and homeless. We can teach the illiterate and stand by the poor who have no one to be a voice for them. Then "gratitude" becomes a possibility not only for those who have an over-abundance of life's necessities but for every person who has a right to the basics of human existence.

 There is so much for which I can give thanks, dear God. Help me to put my gratitude into action.

71

Trusting God for the Rest I Need

> He remained outside in deserted places, and people kept coming to him from everywhere.
>
> MARK
> 1:45

I easily identify with Jesus when he tries to hide out after healing the leper. His hope of finding rest reminds me of the necessity of caring well for one's self and to not get "burned out." Jesus hoped he could get away for some relief, but this time it did not work. People came from everywhere seeking his healing gifts and his pause for rest had to be put on hold. On days when I try to hide out but cannot, I sometimes want to yell, "Leave me alone!" Then I remember this is not how Jesus responded to those who sought him out. He continually turned toward them with compassion. Remembering this helps me to accept those situations that prevent me from getting the solitude and rest my weary self requires.

For each of you who have people who seem never to stop asking or demanding attention when you are exhausted, you who are overburdened and need a break but cannot have it immediately, each of you who yearn to "get away from it all," remember that Jesus has been in that situation. Pray for the strength and resiliency not to cave in, but to hang in there with a gracious response until you find the "deserted place" that your body, mind, and spirit desperately need.

 Jesus, when I remember your response to those in need, I can also be more loving.

when your story and Bible story come together that is the gospel   Doug Bland

Share the Good News of Your Story

When Jesus returned to Capernaum after some days, it became known that he was at home.

MARK 2:1

People managed to quickly spread news about Jesus by word of mouth until the whole countryside was excited about him. We, too, are called to tell the good news. Fear of offending others or doubt about the validity of our spiritual experience can keep us from speaking openly and freely about God. How refreshing it is to hear people relate an event or insight they have had regarding their inner life. How encouraging and inspiring when others share their good news. I think I have been helped more by hearing other people's faith-filled stories than by any theological essay. While we need good theology, even more we need the witness of those who sense divine presence and "know" God through their lived experience. Hearing stories of faith affirms that the Holy One is, indeed, in our midst. Without the good news of life experiences, theology remains dead words on a page.

So the next time you hesitate to speak about God to someone, ask yourself why you are reluctant. Listen to the fears, concerns and any other reasons that keep you silent. Then muster up the humility and courage to spread the good news of your own faith-filled story. Your experience can draw someone else closer to God.

Thank you for the ways you reveal yourself to me, God. Grant me courage to share this revelation when it is appropriate to do so.

Timeworn

For the world in its present form is passing away.

1 CORINTHIANS 7:31

I first understood time as an artificial system when I flew from New Zealand to the U.S. After many hours en route, the flight attendant announced the day and time as we landed. To my surprise, it was still the same day as when I left, even though twenty-four hours had transpired. Crossing the international date line caused us to relive the day. I now look at time differently and am amazed at how we let this human-made structure influence us until we become overwhelmed and almost obsessed with "time."

There is too much time for the ill and lonely, not nearly enough time for the active and busy, too long a time for those waiting for something to happen, too little time for those diagnosed with months to live. How is it we have allowed time to have this much influence over us?

Paul reminds us to keep time in perspective, to see the bigger picture. He nudges us to recall that life consists of impermanence and constant change. All things are truly passing; only the presence of God is enduring. Thus, the question arises: why not focus more attention on this unending love rather than on the overly influential thing we have artificially created and named "time"?

 Instead of looking anxiously at my watch and giving my concerns to the passing of time, let me look at you, Beloved, and enter into your timeless presence.

74

Generosity Costs Less Than It Pays

The measure with which you measure will be measured out to you...
MARK 4:24

A thought-provoking poem by Rabindranath Tagore tells of a beggar at the side of the road who is visited by a king who is on a journey. The king asks the beggar to give him a gift from his tattered bag. The beggar is startled, for he has been thinking that the king will be giving him something rather than asking him for a gift. After all, the beggar has so little. The king has so much. The beggar reluctantly reaches into his bag and pulls out just one kernel of corn and gives it to the king. At the end of the day, when the beggar opens and empties his bag to see what he has gleaned from the day's contributions, he discovers one tiny kernel of gold. Tagore ends the poem with the beggar miserably regretting his failure to give the king all that he had.

I try to remember this powerful message when I am reluctant to give of my presence and talents, when I hold back out of fear or selfishness. Love poured out in full measure will be returned in full measure, maybe not in the manner expected, but it will return in some form of abundance.

 Each day you ask me to share from the wealth of my life, God. Help me to give generously, without resistance or resentment, and to trust that all shall be well.

How Often Do I Sing for Joy?

Then David, girt with a linen apron, came dancing before the Lord with abandon.

2 SAMUEL
6:14

King David accomplished one of the most important actions of his life when he brought the Ark of God into Jerusalem. This ritual was symbolic of the new unity between the fighting religious factions of the north and the south. David and the people were filled with joy, so much so that David was "leaping and dancing before the Lord" (v.16). This joyous celebration of merrymaking and festivity comprised a moment of immense prayer. The festivity demonstrated gratitude and enthusiasm for the presence of God and exhibited the depth of the people's elation.

I ask myself: Do I do anything "with abandon" before my God? Have I ever been that wildly enamored of and grateful for this Gracious One's presence in my life? Does my heart sing with joy? Do my feet lift in happiness? Why is it, I wonder, that I more often pray about pain and troubles than I do about joy and delight? I know my laughter and my enjoyment of life can be as much a prayer as my solemn and somber moments of reflection. King David's enthusiastic response to God has reminded me of this. Today I will look for something to dance about in my prayer.

 Gracious One, may my whole being come to you with abandon as I celebrate your transforming movement in my life.

"Leaving the Scene of Frustration"

[Jesus] sighed from the depth of his spirit...

MARK 8:12

When the Pharisees persisted in arguing with Jesus and pressed him for "a sign from heaven," Jesus emitted a huge sigh—obviously one of exasperation and disappointment. He must have been extremely frustrated with the Pharisees when they harangued him about his teachings. And what does Jesus do after he expresses his frustration? He leaves! He takes off in his boat and goes to another shore.

Are there times when it is legitimate for us to "take off in our boat" and get away from the haranguing and misunderstanding of others? Most certainly. We are not meant simply to accept abusive behavior nor are we to tolerate prejudice and racism. Being Christian doesn't mean that we stop caring for our own well-being or simply dismiss the nastiness of others. Sometimes we need to walk away from what is hurtful and denigrating. Choosing to leave a scene of discouragement or frustration can help us put things in perspective, pray about our emotional response, and regain our self-composure. Leaving the scene is a wise thing to do when we are too irritated to continue the conversation in a loving and peace-oriented manner.

Spirit of Guidance, I count on your wisdom to direct me when I am in a situation where my emotional response is off-balance.

Listening on a Deep Level

Do you have eyes and not see, ears and not hear?

MARK
8:18

When Jesus addressed this question to his disciples, he was commenting on their lack of comprehension about his ministry. His question could be addressed to anyone on most days as none of us are fully aware of the workings of God in our midst. We see and hear on the surface level, but do not always perceive the underlying meaning of events because we are inattentive or not listening with sufficient interest.

Sometimes it takes a big thing to wake us up. I observed this when a 46-year-old woman had a massive stroke. The doctors told her husband she was going to die and he should call the relatives. He did so, but then his wife's condition changed. She came out of the coma, and he was told that the possibility of a complete recovery was good. The husband kept repeating: "It's a miracle. It's like she's been raised from the dead." It did seem that way, after the finality of the physicians' pronouncement.

Eyes to see and ears to hear. Let's notice what is happening in our lives. Let's not wait for a major tragedy to wake us up. Let's not allow life to pass us by while we ignore the signals of divine revelation that come through ordinary and extra-ordinary moments. Let's tune in and be amazed.

May I have clear seeing and keen hearing in order to sense your movement in my life today, God.

How Can I Keep from Singing?

Sing joyfully to the Lord, all you lands...

PSALM 98:4

The psalms often describe nature as giving praise to God. Psalm 98 does so by encouraging all the earth to break into a joyful song. This psalm describes a beautiful scene with the hills singing together and the waves of the sea clapping their hands. This great joy is about the celebrating the beauty and wonder of God. According to the psalmist, it is this divine presence that brings ripples of delight to creation.

The presence of God is everywhere. The more I am aware of this, the more joy my heart contains. The better I listen and more closely I look at where Love is present, the happier I am, the more kindness I generate, the greater peace I experience. It doesn't take much to sing joyfully to God—simply a human heart delighting in the beauty and miracles inherent in every single day: a new leaf on a plant, the lapping of ocean waves on the warm beach, a singing robin, a richly colored sunset, a dancing tree branch. What an immense joy—the gift of being alive and having God with us in each moment of existence. Ah, what joy there is in standing still long enough to discover the splendor in the presence of Love.

 O Beauty ever ancient, ever new, with all of creation I sing the wonder of your love.

79

The Wisdom to Avoid Fighting Back

**But I say
to you,
offer no
resistance
to one who
is evil.**

MATTHEW
5:39

How do we respond to this challenging teaching of Jesus? Most of us are inclined to respond, "yes, but...." Certainly, it is appropriate to stop anyone who commits evil deeds. Jesus did this when he spoke up for those whose lives were in peril. When we are being physically, emotionally, or mentally injured, we have to protect ourselves and try to change situations and systems that hurt ourselves or others.

However, in most situations it is better to offer no resistance. What if I gave a calm rather than angry response when someone is unfairly upset with me? What if I didn't try to verbally overpower those who challenge my beliefs with their denigrating remarks? What if I forgave another who insists that the wrongdoing was all my fault, even if it wasn't? What if I continue to be kind to a person who consistently tries to do me in with nasty comments and vicious gossip? What if I regularly help someone who not only does not say "thank you" but keeps on nagging or ignoring me?

We want to retaliate or resist those who hurt our pride, threaten our security, prey on our vulnerabilities, or simply try to win out over us. Too often we fight back instead of using the gospel approach of offering no resistance.

 God of Peace, guide me in my response to the wrongdoings of others.

80

Faith Shaped by Fire

There appeared the prophet whose words were as a flaming furnace.

SIRACH 48:1

Elijah minced no words when he called the people back to God. His powerful preaching and ardent teaching were often associated with the metaphor of fire. It is said of this prophet that his words "brought down fire" and, when he died, he was "taken aloft in a chariot with fiery horses."

Elijah's words sizzled with intensity and an avid determination to turn people's hearts back to God. Fire is dangerous and must be handled carefully, but it is also purifying and transformative. This zealous and challenging style is not the way I like to learn and grow. Yet there have been times when my strong determination and intense clutching at certain beliefs or behaviors needed to be seared into ashes in order for it to cease. This way of changing my heart usually comes about with my gut response when I hear or read something that first disturbs me, but eventually draws me to see what I must accept for my spiritual transformation.

This way of changing one's heart is not easy but can be highly effective. Approach this fire cautiously, but stay open to what might need to be revealed.

 Fire in My Heart, purify and transform those thoughts and deeds of mine that need changing.

81

Make Amends, Not Excuses

For I acknowledge my offense...
PSALM
51:5

Psalm 51 is a prayer of repentance. It gives us words to acknowledge that we have done wrong, reminding us to do so when our actions require us to ask forgiveness for our attitudes and deeds. We need this prayer because our culture is full of excuses and avoidances, making it seem natural to blame our bad behavior on someone or something else. We find ourselves saying such things as "The words just slipped out. It's my personality style. You're too sensitive. My boss is irritating, and I was upset. I was too tired. I didn't think it would make any difference..."

How blind we can be to the harm we do by our behavior and treatment of others. When we hear ourselves making a lot of excuses for what we've done, it's probably time to turn to Psalm 51 and admit our offenses: "I was wrong. I judged you poorly. I failed to be responsible and thoughtful. I betrayed you by my silence. I was not there for you when you needed me. I was caught up in my self-centeredness. I ignored what I was supposed to do. I deceived you..." And after our acknowledgment of the wrongdoing, come those essential words: "I am sorry. Please forgive me."

 I turn to you, kindhearted God, and ask your forgiveness for when I have failed to be the person you created me to be.

82

What Reward Am I Expecting?

But take care not to perform righteous deeds in order that people may see them...
MATTHEW
6:1

Not being overly concerned about what others think or notice can be enormously difficult. I know that I must consistently check my motivations for what I say and do not say, for what I do and do not do. This need or desire to have my good works noticed and acknowledged can be very subtle. When I do something for someone else and they do not say "thank you," I ask myself how I feel. My emotional response gives me a clue to my motivation for what I have done: if I feel irritated, angry, disappointed, blaming, or impatient for not receiving another's gratitude, I can be quite sure my motivation for doing good was tainted in some way.

Saying "thank you" is an appropriate thing to do. Gratitude is a way to return a kindness. Everyone ought to practice this thoughtful gesture. But when someone does not express thankfulness, then the real opportunity for a genuine good deed occurs: to continue to be generous in spite of the other's lack of gratitude. A good work given with love and without expectation of a reward (not even a "thank you") merits the supreme quality of dedication and devotion that Jesus encouraged of his followers.

 Gracious One, clear my mind and heart of false motivations when I do a good deed for another.

Immense Treasure of God's Love

...and forgive us our debts, as we forgive our debtors...

MATTHEW
6:12

People are especially attentive whenever the topic of forgiveness comes up in retreats and conferences. Countless people experience themselves bearing a grudge toward another, or know of someone who has done so. It is not surprising that deep animosities exist. The more we invest in a relationship or an experience, the more difficult it is to forgive the hurt that comes from that person or experience. Rancor and ill-will build walls of un-forgiveness. The longer the grudge goes on the stronger the wall becomes. Sometimes those who bear grudges actually forget what the initial reason was for shutting out the other person.

Because offering and receiving forgiveness is difficult, we absolutely have to open ourselves to the grace of God. We can't forgive without this help. When we pray to be able to forgive, God can act through us. Another source of help in offering forgiveness is to remember how the Holy One offers us the immense treasure of understanding, hope, and pardon, in spite of our own shortcomings and failures. If we daily open ourselves to the mercy of God welcoming our weak and imperfect selves, we will have the love and mercy to forgive others who have harmed us by their shortcomings and failures.

 Clear away any grudges and non-forgiveness that exist in my heart, Merciful God.

Am I a Living Christian Message?

Do to others whatever you would have them do to you.
MATTHEW 7:1

If you ever wonder whether you are living this core mandate of the gospel, just spend a little time at the end of an especially frustrating day in which everything seemed to fall apart. Take a look and see how you treated each person who entered your life in any way. This look includes those with whom you lived and worked, people you met on the street, subway or bus, every person on the phone, those who waited on you, even people you saw on the daily news or read about in the newspaper. Your response includes your thoughts and feelings as well as your manner of acting. Did you ignore anyone? Refuse to talk to them? Judge negatively or harshly? Feel a bit of envy, anger, or spite? Push your way ahead? Talk endlessly about yourself? Feel superior to someone? Wish them ill? Speak grumpily?

How many of your responses would you want others to extend to you? If you treated everyone the way you want to be treated, then the teaching of Jesus is undoubtedly alive and well in you. If not, it may well be time to renew your efforts to live the Christian message.

 Jesus, when I fail to do unto others as I want them to do to me, grant me courage and hope to begin again the next day with a renewed intention to live your gospel of love.

Prayer Sends Us Forth

It is too little [the Lord] says, for you to be my servant, to raise up the tribes of Jacob, and restore the survivors of Israel; I will make you a light to the nations, that my salvation may reach to the ends of the earth.

ISAIAH
49:6

Prayer is meant to "grow us." Every divine encounter holds the possibility of transforming us a bit more. Genuine prayer is risky. It changes us, and we are never sure what that change might be. We may not initially be aware of the alteration within our self because these movements are often imperceptible, but each authentic prayer reveals more of our truest self. Each genuine prayer has an effect in how we live. This transformation includes discovering our preeminent virtues and our most dismal compulsions, our finest qualities and our most embarrassing traits.

The changes within us are not just for our self. Rather than our relationship with God isolating us, it connects us more fully with the larger dimension of life. The influence of our prayer carries over into the world in which we are a part. When we leave our place of prayer, the Spirit sends us forth to live as persons of great love. Our heart "knows"—has faith—that Someone greater than ourselves sends us onward.

 When we meet in prayer, draw me ever closer to you, Beloved. Then, urge me to go forth to bring your love into the world.

God Knows the Good in Me

You have probed me and you know me.

PSALM
139:1

When I was younger, I found it scary to consider that God might know me through and through. Now, at this stage of my life, I find considerable comfort in the thought. What changed for me? In the past, I definitely did not want God sneaking a peek into my inner closet full of bad habits or my inner basement crammed with self-centered projects and false judgments. When I learned to accept my less-than-perfect-self, my discomfort with God's knowing me as I am was disarmed. When this happened, I realized God knew who I was all along and was quite willing to have me as I am. I also found comfort in accepting that God believes in my full potential for love and will help me to live it. Author Anne Lamott suggests, "God loves you just as you are, and God loves you too much to let you stay that way."

While my need to grow continues, I am no longer afraid of God knowing every part of my self. I trust there is an essence of intrinsic goodness at the core of my being. I believe this for everyone. The more we know and accept ourselves for who we are, the more we trust God to probe any part of our life and never give up on us. What a relief!

 Take me as I am, Loving God, and grow me into who I am yet to become.

Our Only Help When Swamped

I am sunk in the abysmal swamp where there is no foothold.

PSALM
69:3

An abysmal swamp is a murky, scary place to be, especially when there's no place to gain a footing for balance and get out of the water. If a person cannot swim, a huge fear of drowning naturally arises. The psalmist named well what many of us feel at certain times. We may not be in the physical waters of a swamp, but we can feel pulled under the grimy waters of busyness, relationship difficulties, loneliness, grief, physical pain, emotional distress, joblessness, and anything else that threatens our peace of mind and heart. At these times, we, too, are desperate to gain a foothold to get out of the struggle.

Being in this sort of abysmal swamp may actually provide a spiritual gift if it forces us back into the arms of God. There's nowhere else to go except to the One who can give us the strength and courage to endure the swamp of our distress. When we feel about to go under, we can cry out with the psalmist, "Let your saving help, O God, protect me" (Psalm 69:30). Then we more fully understand who and what truly matters in our life.

When I get caught in the abysmal swamp, God, I will reach out my hand toward you with hope. I trust that I will receive what I need to make it out of the swamp.

The Many Ways of Naming God

God replied, "I am who I am."

EXODUS 3:14

I will be who I will be. Waskow (handwritten)

Christianity, along with other major religions, suggests a great diversity of designations and qualities for God. St. Thomas Aquinas developed a litany of titles, all taken from the Jewish and Christian Scriptures. Muslims chant "the 99 most beautiful names," and Hindus recite "the 1000 names of the divine." One ancient source refers to God's infinite amount of characteristics by noting that "God has a million faces."

"I am who I am" encompasses all the titles ever used to describe the tremendous presence of the divine being, yet when Jesus came along he chose to speak of his Beloved with a variety of names and qualities, including the gentle one of "Abba," the tender parent. From his own humanness, Jesus knew that we needed something a bit more tangible to convey this sacred relationship. Discovering and naming divinity in diverse ways awakens and enriches our relationship. Today you might think about what name most adequately describes how you currently experience "I am who I am." Perhaps "Patient One," "Generosity," "Trusted Confidant," "All-Forgiving Friend," or "Hidden Presence" might be among your choices.

Thank you for being such an intimate part of my life, You-Who-Have-Countless-Names. Each way of speaking to you gives me another opportunity to relate to you.

A Difficult Teaching

Love your enemies, and pray for those who persecute you...
MATTHEW 5:44

Some teachings of Jesus I would like to ignore. Praying for those who persecute me is one of them. There are people whose lives are in daily danger due to enemies who would torture or kill them because of their way of life or personal beliefs. For most of us the kind of maltreatment we experience is less deadly and more subtle. These actions can still maim our spirit, however. We are "persecuted" when people try to deliberately cause pain for us, when they try to inflict hurt with false accusations or cruel rumors, with angry silence or nasty put-downs, with hostile looks or demeaning deeds.

When I experience someone intentionally against me, my first response is to act in a similar manner. Jesus does not say we are to remain in a situation where we are "persecuted." What he does tell us is to remember that divine love is stronger than the desire to hate. We are to continue to care about and to pray for those who seek to wound us. With God's grace, we can give up our desire for revenge, a response that only serves to shape our heart into angry aggression and stony resentment.

 Soften my heart, Loving God, when the behavior of others toward me arouses a desire to harden my heart.

Spiritual Cleansing

Wash yourselves clean!

ISAIAH
1:16

Many religious traditions use various aspects of cleanliness as a metaphor for spiritual purity. This metaphor signifies the washing away of sinful ways, the purifying of one's thoughts and attitudes, the cleansing of old habits that draw one away from living as a friend of God. Physical cleanliness is not much of a problem for those who have access to washing machines and dishwashers. Spiritual cleanliness, on the other hand, is not so easily remedied or efficient. When we strive to rid ourselves of what keeps us from living the teachings of Jesus, we must make a deliberate effort to do so. This cleansing requires persistence and determination, a lot of spiritual "elbow grease," a day-to-day vigilance, and a desire to change.

Like dishes and clothes that continually need washing, so too with spiritual cleanliness. Just when I think I have mastered my dreadful habits and cleansed my thoughts, words, and deeds, I can find myself repeating them again. It would be easy to get discouraged with this undulating pattern if it were not for the truth of God's mercy and forgiveness. With God's grace, I know I always have another chance to "wash myself clean" if I am willing to give myself to the process.

 As I wash my body today, God, I turn my heart to you with a prayer that you will aid the cleansing of my inner self.

Leaving Behind What Enslaves Us

They had been rushed out of Egypt and had no opportunity even to prepare food for the journey.

EXODUS
12:39

How quickly the Israelites departed from Egypt when the call came to "go." They left their homes so hastily there was no time to prepare food. They heard the call to freedom and responded wholeheartedly. This movement toward physical freedom parallels the journey to spiritual freedom, that inner place where we are at home with both self and God. The Holy One continues to call people out of places of spiritual enslavement. Each of us is regularly asked to leave the "Egypt" of our own making, whether this "Egypt" consists of unloving behaviors, destructive habits, negative attitudes or anything else that keeps us from being our best self.

When the call of God urges us to leave what keeps us enslaved, it's time to go. We may be reluctant to leave those things behind. A part of us lags back, questions, resists, and does not want to put forth the effort to move toward what will truly free us. I remember a time when I was enslaved by my criticism of others. One day I heard how destructive my comments were. It was difficult to leave the easy satisfaction those critical remarks gave me. Eventually, I moved out of my "Egypt," but in the time it took to do so I could have prepared a lot of food!

 Free me from what keeps my heart from being fully yours, O God.

God Is Near Even in My Dark Nights

My soul yearns for you in the night...
ISAIAH
26:9

The nighttime of our lives is often when we most long for a taste of God's presence to dispel the bleakness of our inner landscape. In those moments we are least likely to have a sense of this consoling presence. I have experienced this inner, barren landscape myself, as have most of the women and men who come to me for spiritual guidance. When we are depressed, experiencing adversity, or overwhelmed with loss or pain, we seem to lose a closeness with God. Instead of sensing the warmth of consolation, we feel only an empty, hollow space echoing our cry for relief.

These experiences of barrenness and darkness cause our soul to seek a taste of consolation and an assurance regarding God's abiding presence. Everything in us longs for some validation that we have not been abandoned. Hidden in this nighttime desolation, of course, is the truth that God remains near to us, never for a moment letting us out of Love's compassionate embrace or vigilant sight. If only we could remember this when we cry out in our pain and wonder if we have been left alone in our misery. Here is where the core of faith receives its great challenge. For now is the time to continue to pray and not give up hope, in spite of seemingly having nothing in response.

 Abiding Presence, deepen my faith when you seem far from me.

God's Mercy Is Infinite

With age-old love I have loved you; so I have kept my mercy toward you.

JEREMIAH
31:3

An age-old love endures no matter what the situation. The Hebrew word for this kind of love is hesed. This word translates as either "mercy, compassion, or kindness." What the translations do not include is the fuller meaning, that hesed actually implies excessive mercy, compassion, and kindness, far beyond what the human mind can grasp, or believes is possible. Hesed is love that overflows with acceptance and kindheartedness.

We humans do not fully realize the vastness of God's mercy. We are too easily swept away with our judgments of both self and others, too quick to condemn and want retribution for those who deliberately hurt us or others. We want to be assured that they've paid the price for their harmful actions and have proven their willingness to change before we approach them with anything other than disdain or contempt.

Not so with God's mercy. Here the message is "Come. You always have a welcome with me. I forgive you. I believe in your goodness. I will wait for you to grow and change and, while I do, I accept you with all my heart."

 God of excessive mercy, I want to be filled with this same kind of mercy. I want to offer your kind of welcome and forgiveness.

94

Keep on Keeping on

For the vision still has its time, presses on to fulfillment, and will not disappoint.

HABAKKUK
2:3

The prophet Habakkuk questioned God, demanding answers for why Judah was still filled with social abuse and corruption. God met Habakkuk's complaints with an answer we need to hear in today's world. God encouraged the prophet not to lose heart and told him that even if what he hoped for was delayed, he should "wait for it, for it will surely come...."

If we pay attention to most any aspect of world news, we know the challenge of God's message to Habakkuk. A dedicated peace advocate recently asked me: "Do you think we will ever have world peace?" I remembered God's word to Habakkuk. It helped me reply without hesitation, "Yes. I do not know when or how, but someday our world will have peace."

If we lose our vision, we lose our hope. When this happens, we give ourselves over to a bleak, meaningless existence where we waste our valuable gifts and talents that could help necessary change take place. Whether we wait for changes in our personal life, the Church, or the world, we need to maintain and nurture our vision of what is to come. It will come, in a time and manner we least expect.

 Restore my vision and strengthen my hope when these precious items begin to limp, God. Teach me what you would have me be or do in order to enable the vision to become a reality.

Memories Can Be Tools for Growth

Think back on the days of old, reflect on the years of age upon age.
DEUTERONOMY
32:7

Increasingly I appreciate the value of reflecting on my life to see what I can learn from it. In doing so, I see my story intertwined with The Holy One. I recognize the way God was guiding and guarding, encouraging and consoling, inspiring and inspiriting me. I sense an immense gratitude as I recall what helped me to grow. I recognize events and relationships that surprised and blessed me. I also see patterns of thought and living that held me back from spiritual growth. Getting in touch with these dimensions helps me to see where I still need healing and continued conversion.

Having learned this helpful approach for myself, I often suggest it to others as a tool for spiritual growth. This process consists of gathering memories, browsing through one's life in decades or "ages" (childhood, adolescence, young adult) and writing down phrases for whatever comes to mind from that era of life. Then, perusing the memories with two questions in mind: "How was God with me during this time? Which of these memories show me where I need to still grow spiritually?" Conclude the review by writing a renewed commitment to God.

 Eternal Companion, you steadfastly journey with me and help me to grow through every step of my life.

A Strong and Enduring Faith

O woman, great is your faith!

MATTHEW
15:28

The Canaanite woman begs Jesus to heal her child. Surprisingly, Jesus ignores her urgent appeal, turning aside and appearing indifferent to her beseeching plea. "He did not say a word in answer to her" (verse 23). This mother does not give up, so strong is her love for her daughter and her belief that Jesus can heal. She's willing to grovel in order to find help for her ill child and continues to insist that he do so as she implores a response from him.

So where is the compassionate Christ, the one who readily heals those in need? How could he turn aside from the pleadings of this distressed mother? When Jesus deliberately acts contrary to his usual response of healing, he seemingly does so in order to use the moment as a time to teach. After he heals the child, Jesus turns to the woman and affirms the quality of her faith. I have often wondered about this story, but now I see it as a lesson in not giving up, in trusting. What we pray for and desire does not take place in our time frame nor always with the response we expect. Like the Canaanite woman, we keep longing and hoping when all seems in vain. Deep faith is a tough virtue to attain.

 Healing Christ, when I question the worth of my prayers, reinforce my faith and strengthen my trust in you.

"Stuck in the Sludge of Life"

Jeremiah sank into the mud.

JEREMIAH
38:6

When the enemies of the prophet Jeremiah got fed up with his challenging messages of repentance, they shoved him into a cistern, hoping to get rid of him. Fortunately, the cistern had only mud in it so he did not drown. Eventually Jeremiah was pulled out.

Sinking into the mud—we have all been there. When people or events get the best of us or when our own wily ways nab us, we can easily sink into the mud of discouragement. This quagmire includes things like anxiety, self-doubt, lack of concern for others, loneliness, fear, self-righteousness, revenge, hostility, and self-pity.

Sinking into the mud is not an entirely awful place to be if it affords us the opportunity and time to get some distance and objectivity about our problems. Sometimes being stuck in the sludge of life is the only thing that can make us realize how much we need God. Eventually, we have to get out of the mud. Just as Jeremiah could not make it out all by himself, neither can we. We are pulled out by the kindness of those who care, the grace of God's help, and the persistence of daily prayer.

 When I get caught in the sludge of my life, God, you are there with me, as both my encourager and my teacher.

Trustworthy Shepherds

Thus says the Lord God: I myself will look after and tend my sheep.

EZEKIEL
34:11

Most people today are unfamiliar with the rural profession of shepherding, but in earlier times it provided an excellent metaphor for both prophets and Jesus to describe God's care for us and how we are to do the same. Good shepherds guide and guard their sheep, leading them to nourishing pastures, making sure they do not come to harm. The divine shepherd does the same for the human flock, often doing so through the graced way that people treat one another.

Last year I relearned this through a man at a retreat. He told me how my aunt and uncle shepherded him at a time in his young life when he was lost and in need of help. When he was down and out, they took him into their home. There he experienced guiding direction, compassionate attention, and generous shelter. They led him away from past hurts and supplied nourishment for his body and spirit. We can all be trustworthy shepherds whether we are parents, teachers, nurses, pastoral ministers, counselors, grandparents, or anyone considerate enough to act for the well-being of another. It takes some effort to go beyond egocentricity and concern for self-welfare in order to be a "good shepherd." That's why we continually re-turn our focus to the Good Shepherd's teachings and example.

 Dear God, as you shepherd my heart and care for me each day, may I do the same for others.

Count on God's Grace

A clean heart create for me, O God...

PSALM
51:12

Notice that the Bible verse does not say "help me create a clean heart." Rather, the psalmist implies that God is the one who effectively cleans up the mess inside. Certainly we need to do our part in getting rid of the inner residue of old hurts, damaging attitudes, self-deprecating talk, grudging bitterness, and any mental or emotional clutter that keeps us from being our best self. But the reality is that we cannot do any of this by our effort alone. The psalmist points this out clearly.

In spite of this reality, I continually get caught in the mind-set of thinking I can manage my spiritual growth by myself. Part of this thinking is due to my personality and part is due to the western culture that consistently urges a do-it-yourself approach. Fortunately, God continues to move in our lives in spite of this mentality.

The Holy One helps clean our soiled heart through pricks of conscience, those unsettling nudges to change our ways, and the sharp reminders (often by the very people we dislike) to consider revising our way of responding to life. If we desire to transform our heart into one of great love, we can count on God's grace to help us with this daunting task.

 Create a clean heart for me, O God, for I cannot do this all by myself.

All Are Invited to the Table

Go out, therefore, into the main roads and invite to the feast whomever you find.
MATTHEW 22:9

Have you ever thought about the people who came to the feast after others excused themselves and refused to accept the invitation? This parable tells us that "the servants went out into the streets and gathered all they found, bad and good alike, and the hall was filled with guests" (verse 10). We each have our own idea of who these "bad" people from the byways might be. They're probably the very people we would not want to have eating with us at our table. Anyone we do not want at the table of life with us is the very person whom Jesus invites to be there. Those who do not "fit in" or who are on the margins of life will definitely be included.

Jesus insisted all the guests have a wedding garment that, in this parable, symbolizes repentance. None of us can give up on ourselves, or on anyone else. We all need to be allowed room to change our ways. We ought not to categorize others or turn our backs on anyone because, as this parable teaches, the very people we term "bad" are the ones God seats at the table when the great invitation comes. Let's open our minds and hearts a little wider today to include those we push to the edges of our acceptance.

 Loving God, keep me open to your presence in each person I meet today.

We Can't Have Too Much Gratitude

I will thank you always for what you have done...
PSALM
52:11

I don't think we can have too much gratitude. When a dear friend of mine died of a brain tumor, one of the most important things she left behind for me was her consistent practice of being grateful. Life was not always easy for her. Sandra had her share of discouragement, irritation and hard times, but no matter how tough things were, she could find something for which to be grateful. When she was in hospice and became dependent physically, she'd say, "These nurses are so kind to me." When she had endless back pain from lying in bed, she would look out the window and exclaim: "The sky is beautiful today." When visitors called or came, Sandra always made a point of thanking them for taking time for her. She did not deny the tough aspects of her condition but she chose to look beyond or beneath them, to find what might bring some joy amid her unchangeable difficulties.

"Being grateful" makes all the difference in how each day unfolds. If I enter the morning feeling disgruntled, I can find all sorts of things to complain about throughout the day. If, instead, I acknowledge my grouchiness and then set my intention to find what is good in the day, my attitude changes and I can almost always find something for which to be grateful.

 Forgive me, Generous Creator, for the times my heart lacks gratitude.

Making Myself Aware of God's Mercy

...for his mercy endures forever.

PSALM
136:1

The above refrain is proclaimed twenty-six times in Psalm 136 in honor of God's mercy. I used to wonder why the phrase was continually repeated until I realized that the psalmist was emphasizing the endlessness of God's mercy by this constant repetition. The recurring praise of God's mercy is a valuable reminder of the countless times the Holy One has welcomed us back after we have wandered and fallen from the path of goodness. The repetition also serves to convince us that God's mercy will continually be available to us whenever we turn toward this Enduring Love and ask forgiveness for our failings.

I suggest that each of us reflect back on the mistakes, deliberate wrongdoings, poor judgments and decisions we have made that have hurt ourselves or others. After each item that we recall, we can then say: "for your mercy endures forever." By doing so, we will see that our whole life consists of a psalm praising the mercy and kindness of God, extended to us at every moment. This litany of mercy can be a powerful experience for anyone who doubts that they are eternally embraced in the Divine Forgiver's arms.

 Compassionate One, may the mercy you daily offer me be an incentive to also extend kindness and forgiveness to those who have wronged or failed me.

103

A Mystery Too Deep for Words

Among human beings, who knows what pertains to a person except the spirit of the person that is within? Similarly, no one knows what pertains to God except the Spirit of God.

1 CORINTHIANS 2:11

Can you think of anyone you know thoroughly? Me neither. Even couples who have lived together over fifty years, who are familiar with each other's thoughts and gestures, can still be surprised by some aspect of their spouse. None of us knows entirely "what pertains to a person."

This is all the more true regarding the mystery of God. We may think we have a fine grasp of what there is to know about this immense Being, but truly, our knowledge is only a speck of who this vast treasure is. People who speak as if they know everything about God limit the richness of divinity.

Although I align my understanding of divinity with what Scripture and my life experiences tell me about divinity, this awareness falls far short of the fathomless bounty of this endless goodness. While it is helpful to designate names and qualities of God so we can relate personally to this great mystery, we must humbly admit that "no one knows what pertains to God except the Spirit of God."

 Even though I know only a tiny portion of who you are, God, I love what I do understand and experience of you in my life.

Resting in God

Only in God be at rest, my soul...

PSALM 62:6

Some writers on meditation encourage their readers to "rest in God." Doing nothing in prayer except resting in God sounds extremely satisfying and comfortable, kind of like pulling up a beach chair by the side of a lovely lake or ocean and taking it easy. Probably most of us would like nothing more than to do this when we pray. The thought of resting like this is enticing. Then why is it so difficult? Why do we find it challenging to just "be" with the One who claims our heart? What causes us to squirm around when we have nothing to do but be present?

We forget about preparation. There are actions to take before we get to the comfy beach chair — canceling appointments, packing some food and drink, driving to the beach, getting a parking place, setting up our chair, and putting on sunscreen. In the same way, coming to a place of rest in God takes preparation — setting aside a definite time each day, finding a relatively quiet place, resisting answering the phone, and setting aside the big list of "have to do" items. After this is done, we then breathe a sigh of relief, entrust our life to God and enjoy the wonderful "rest" without thinking we have to have something to show for our efforts after our time with the Holy One is completed.

 Help me to rest in you, my Beloved.

Labeling Others Unfairly

...and Judas Iscariot, who became a traitor.

LUKE
6:16

Do you consider Judas Iscariot as anything but a traitor? Do you think of him also as someone who was a son, a neighbor, a coworker, a friend? Probably not. Isn't it something how quickly people get labeled and are unable to get rid of the negative image others have of them? Judas did a horrible thing in betraying Jesus. He also regretted his sinfulness, returned the betrayal money, and confessed he had sinned. Few in history remember Judas for these things, only his disastrous deed.

It's easy for me to label people who harm others as horrible persons. How quickly I forget that these persons I've labeled as "bad" also have families and friends who care about them. How readily I dismiss the possibility that I might not know the full story behind that person's life or behavior. This does not mean that I excuse what has been done but it does imply that beneath the action there is a human being whom God created and loves as fully as God loves me. Labeling others in any way keeps me from being open to the fullness of who they are. It shuts the door to the possibility of their growth and conversion. It keeps them in my small box of judgment and withholds the Gospel treasures of compassion and forgiveness.

 God of forgiveness, free me from labeling others and withholding my compassion from them.

Pray and Ponder

While [Jesus] was going through a field of grain on a Sabbath, his disciples were picking the heads of grain, rubbing them in their hands, and eating them.

LUKE
6:1

As a Jew, Jesus was limited in the activities he could do on the Sabbath. Picking and eating grain implied harvesting and was seen as a type of work. Laboring on the Sabbath was not one of the approved behaviors of his religion. Jesus had the courage to challenge openly the tightly boxed-in regulations. He did so partly because the rules had lessened in value and meaning. Jesus respected laws, such as the Great Commandment. He did not dismiss the law lightly, but he knew when it was appropriate to set the law aside. Scripture tells us that Jesus spent long hours of the night in reflective prayer. Although the Gospels do not tell us what Jesus prayed about, surely his struggle with the overemphasis on religious law was part of his contemplative discernment.

Whenever we meet with confusion in our personal lives, we can follow the example of Jesus. Like him, we do not figure out answers to our concerns by ourselves. We take them to prayer and ponder them at length. We listen to our inner Wisdom and to the good judgment of others. Then we collect our courage and do what is required for our spiritual growth.

 When I struggle with decisions to be made, I will turn to you, Guide of my life.

107

Finding the "Immense Calm" Within

...that we may lead a quiet and tranquil life in all devotion and dignity.
1 TIMOTHY 2:2

In his letter to Timothy, Paul requests prayers for everyone, suggesting that these prayers will help us to lead "a quiet and tranquil life." Is Paul saying that people with passion and robust enthusiasm are not leading a spiritual life or that prayer will protect us from experiencing problems? I think not. The amount of activity or the number of problem-free days we have is not what affects our relationship with God, nor is it to be the expected outcome of prayer. Rather, the effect of prayer is whether or not we allow the Immense Calm within us to move us toward peace instead of hostility, love rather than alienation, reconciliation in place of discord, compromise rather than stubborn individualism.

At the heart of who we are there is a quiet place where we can go amidst all sorts of energetic or disruptive life events. We can return time and again to this core of God's peace at the center of our being. Then, no matter how ruffled the feathers of our daily schedule might get, we can be united and guided by the One who is our tower of strength and our placid lake of calm.

 Peacemaker and Quiet of my heart, when life roller coasters with activity, draw me back to the depths of my heart where you dwell in stillness.

Delighting in the Exquisite

Great are the works of the Lord, exquisite in all their delights.

PSALM
111:2

When I pondered this beautiful psalm verse, I thought to myself: "When is the last time I thought of something God created as exquisite?" As I reflected on this, all sorts of marvelous things tumbled into my mind. Here are some of them: the spiritual growth I witness in those who come for spiritual guidance; the way the little creek fills up and flows along merrily in heavy rains; the busy nuthatch hanging upside down on the maple branch; the sliver of waning moon with a shining planet beside it in the night sky; the deep wrinkles on the wise visage of an older person's face; the compassionate way hospice workers accompany the dying; the innocence of young children who are totally open; the way words sometimes fall in amazing patterns onto the page; the graced ability of another to love me unconditionally.

What is exquisite in your world? Who and what delights you? When have you last paused to look closely at the environment in which you live? How have the great works of the Creator brought you happiness and joy? Are you able to give yourself permission to gaze with wonder? Look around and notice. Then speak your gratitude to the One who gives us everything that is exquisite.

 Author of all that exists, today I will look with awe and renewed attention to everything that is a part of my life.

Following without Knowing the Way

He saw a man named Matthew sitting at the customs post. He said to him, "Follow me."

MATTHEW 9:9

Matthew heard not only an external voice but something far deeper. Because of this inner resonance, Matthew got up and followed the One who called, and his life was never the same. Little did he know at that time how his life would unfold. What courage and trust it must have taken to walk into the mystery of life so fully. Like Matthew, we are each called to daily "leave all and follow." Just the other day someone in the middle of an intense spiritual growth issue said to me, "What makes this process so challenging is that I have no idea what might come from it. It's scary. I don't know how God might lead me to change if I continue to stay with this journey."

The truth is that none of us knows where we are going to be led once we "get up and follow" the Spirit's voice of invitation and guidance. In her book, *I'd Say "Yes" God, If I Knew What You Wanted*, Nancy Reeves encourages her readers to "make the decision that seems best to you. And remember that God does not leave in disgust when we make a mistake. If we are receptive, mistakes make great learning experiences."

 I place my trust in you, Divine Companion, as I travel life's path.

What's in Your Heart?

Plot no evil against your neighbor...
PROVERBS
3:29

The thought of deliberately scheming and planning evil against someone leaves most of us aghast. We would not think of doing something that deceitful or damaging. Yet planning harm might be more prevalent than one wants to believe. I've known those who connived to gain an inheritance for themselves and foil it for others, coworkers who destroyed another's good name by deliberately spreading false rumors, friends whose jealousy contributed to the breakup of a marriage, parents who suffered long years because of a child's refusal to forgive.

There's another aspect to this proverb. Maybe we do not purposefully plot evil, but we can act smugly, self-righteously savoring the result of another's bad behavior. When I grew up, it was quite common if something disastrous happened to certain questionable people to hear comments such as, "He asked for it." "She should have known better." "They got what was coming to them." Even now I occasionally catch myself thinking of some awful thing I wouldn't mind having befall someone whom I consider a danger to society. That's why I stay in touch with my deeper self each day to see what's going on in there.

 God of Love, lead me each day to search my heart and observe if your ways are my ways, if I am as loving as you desire me to love.

Going from Hurt to Healing Is Slow

Those that sow in tears shall reap rejoicing.

PSALM
126:5

The journey from tears to rejoicing quite often takes much longer than the grieving one anticipates. The going from sowing to reaping that the psalmist speaks of is a gradual process of transformation. When a seed is sown it does not spring up quickly into a thriving plant. Each seed has its own gestation period and cannot be rushed. The movement from spring planting to autumn harvesting takes time for maturation to occur. The reaping of fruits, nuts and vegetables only comes about after the crops have been carefully tended.

The same is true for each of us and our journeys from sorrow to joy. We cannot force or hurry the healing of our bodies, minds, and spirits, even though we want to leave the pain and distress behind as quickly as possible. We are apt to forget this when we, or others, are moving from hurt to healing. During certain times of my sorrow, I have actually planted a seed and watched its slow but deliberate movement into life. This did not take my heartache away but it eased my impatience with the gradual process of healing and strengthened my trust that eventually my tears would lessen and my joy increase.

 May those who are sowing in tears this day turn to you, Sower of Joy. Restore their hope and ease their sorrows.

112

Spiritual Prosperity of Our Work

Prosper the work of our hands for us!
PSALM
90:17

Think of what you accomplish in one day with the use of your hands. Imagine your life if you did not have these two magnificent gifts. How different life would be without the mobility and dexterity of our hands. These helpful parts of the body symbolize various aspects of "work," including service, hospitality, giving and receiving, caring, and generosity.

When "work" thrives, more happens than financial success or affirmation of our achievements. We know our work prospers when the best of who we are comes forth, when what we do benefits not only ourselves but others, when the results of our labor bring wisdom and guidance for the next generation, as well as protecting and sustaining what is essential for the good health of our planet.

One of the ways to ensure that our work flourishes is by continually rededicating all we are and do to the One who helps our work succeed. As the Jewish philosopher Martin Buber wisely stated, "It is not the nature of our work, but its consecration that is the vital thing." As we go about our activities today, may the quality with which we do them reflect the desires of God for our world.

 Loving God, may I be aware of how the work of my hands helps the physical, mental, spiritual, and emotional well-being of myself and others.

113

Examining My Motives

"Who then is this about whom I hear such things?" And [Herod] kept trying to see [Jesus].

LUKE
9:9

Motivation is a significant factor underlying our behavior. It tells us whether what we do is reflective of the gospel teachings or not. Herod wanted to see Jesus, not because he thought Jesus might be someone who could have a positive influence on his life, but because he thought Jesus was drawing people away from him and usurping royal power. Herod's action was deceitful because his motivation was distorted. He acted out of self-centeredness and insecurity, not out of genuine curiosity and hospitality.

I recently read about Tom White, a quiet philanthropist whose motivation reflects humble integrity. White has unobtrusively given away over fifty million dollars, mainly to help low-income people and those working for justice. He has done so without seeking attention or expecting gratitude. Not many people can be that ego-less and clear-hearted.

When I think about Herod's motives, I am led to be more attentive to my own motivations: Are my desires and actions due to a need to be recognized, to cover up guilt, to pacify hurt feelings, to be thanked, to establish a sense of superiority? Or am I striving to do good simply because this approach reflects what Jesus lived and taught? Always the question behind my actions is the "why" of what I do.

 Spirit of God, keep me honest in all I am and all I do.

Acknowledging My Need for God

I fell on my knees, stretching out my hands to the Lord, my God.

EZRA
9:5

An Interrupted Life, the diaries of Etty Hillesum, a Jewish woman who died at Auschwitz at the age of twenty-nine, inspires me toward greater recognition of all God does for me. Etty's entries candidly reveal her developing relationship with God. As she is caught in the Holocaust, Etty inches closer and closer to the One whom she searched for and desired to know in her earlier, unsettled years. Gradually, Etty surrenders her heart to God, growing certain that whatever happens, the Holy One is near. A significant aspect of this relationship is revealed when Etty reflects on feeling called to kneel. She writes: "Sometimes, in moments of deep gratitude, kneeling down becomes an overwhelming urge, head deeply bowed, hands before my face."

The prophet Ezra's kneeling is about humble repentance. In Etty's case, it is the only way she can fully express how she feels about God's loving presence, humble gratitude and reverence. Her words remind me that whether we physically kneel is not nearly as important as our kneeling inwardly. What matters is whether we acknowledge our complete dependency upon God to grow and change us, to lead us into a love that knows no conditions or bounds, just as Jesus came to his own peace when he surrendered to God in the Garden of Olives.

 My well-being and transformation depends upon you, God. Thank you.

Peace Comes and Peace Goes

In this place I will give peace, says the Lord of hosts!
HAGGAI
2:9

Peace comes when we are at home with who we are and how we are, no matter what conditions of our life. This inner harmony is not an effortless accomplishment. We are often at peace one day and not the next. Unfortunately, we can easily allow life's ups and downs to steal peace from us. Much of our inner atmosphere depends on how we draw upon our faith and whether we lessen our control on making life evolve according to our expectations. Peace flows steadily in the heart when there is acceptance.

A recent letter taught me a lot about how one can live peacefully even though life is not all one hopes it to be. My correspondent was a man who has lived with the mental illness of schizophrenia for years. While medication usually keeps his illness in check, it does not cure him of it. The letter was not directly about his illness, but this man openly included some details about this aspect of his life. I was touched by his willingness to do so and felt blessed to know someone who is at peace with his mental condition. Unfortunately, too many people in our society still see mental illness as a stigma and think less of themselves or others who are afflicted in this way.

 Healing Christ, may your compassionate presence be a source of peace for those with illness of any kind.

116

Keep Your Focus on What Is of Value

...the Lord appointed seventy [-two] others whom he sent ahead of him in pairs to every town and place he intended to visit.

LUKE
10:1

Jesus sends his disciples out in pairs, rather than one by one, to prepare the way for him. Jesus clearly knows the benefits of being with someone else who shares the urgency of his mission and the focus of his message. He urges them to take very little with them, to live simply. By doing so, Jesus encourages them not to get distracted by anything else. He is saying, "You have one another and you have my belief in you. Do not be waylaid by getting too much stuff that can sidetrack and disorient you. Keep your focus on what is truly of value."

Jesus sends these disciples ahead of him to open minds and soften hearts, to ready others to hear and receive his message. He tells them to move on when they are not well received so they will not get caught up in useless arguments and volatile rhetoric. Rather, they are to carry the message with loving hearts, clear minds, a day-to-day peacefulness, and non-attachment to material things. Surely this kind of discipleship is possible for us as well as we, too, daily enter into relationship with our wise teacher of love.

 Great Teacher, I want to be your disciple and learn from you. Help me to do so.

No More Being Too Nice with God

Yes, it is near, a day of darkness and of gloom, a day of clouds and somberness!

JOEL
2:2

Through the ages, hurting people have raised their anguished voices to God. These voices have been filled with agonizing questions, tearful requests, and angry accusations. They have implored, begged, and pleaded for relief or for answers. They have cried out in pain and sought solace by voicing their emotions. Scriptural passages are filled with these prayers, thus assuring us it is all right to cry out to the Holy One.

I used to be too nice with God when I was feeling desolate about painful life events. I now realize that not being honest with my divine companion about my situation only added to the soreness of my emotional state. Trying to hide the hurt, avoiding the reality of my discomfort when I was at prayer benefited no one and only generated more self-pity and resentment.

I do not believe that God sends suffering. Suffering happens because of our human condition, the choices we make, and because of the way transformation evolves with its growthful cycle of life-death-life. Still, this truth does not take away my human, emotional response that sometimes includes the dimension of emotional pain. Nor does it cease my silent hope that my communication with God will make a difference.

 Loving God, you know me through and through. Let me not hide from you, or from myself, the feelings that arise within me.

118

Welcoming Strangers

Has none but this foreigner returned to give thanks to God?

LUKE
17:18

Not long ago I passed a homeless man standing on a street corner, talking to himself. I wondered about his life story and what sustained him interiorly. The gospel story today is also about strangers. Did Jesus question who the ten lepers were when they cried out to be healed? Did he insist on knowing how they contracted the disease or if they had taken good enough care of themselves? He seems not to have been concerned about their personal history, religion, or ethnicity, but immediately heals the lepers when he encounters them.

At the same time, Jesus takes special notice of the foreigner who returns to give thanks. He commends the person for his faith, perhaps to point out the inner goodness of the man to the bystanders. As with the leper, or the homeless person on a street corner, we do not know what stirs within the stranger's heart. What we do know is that there is still far too much bias, prejudice, false judgment, and intolerance in our world.

This gospel story leads me into my own heart to ask: Am I open and welcoming to those who are hurting in any way? Am I willing to receive them without judgment as Jesus received the ten lepers and be a source of loving presence to them?

 Gracious One, change the hearts of all of us who cling to harmful biases and prejudices.

119

Face Guilt, Don't Cover It Up

Then I acknowledged my sin to you, my guilt I covered not.
PSALM
32:5

Guilt is sometimes beneficial for our spiritual growth. The gnawing feeling that arises when we choose to be less than our true self can be a healthy emotional response. We may need to forgive ourselves, or ask forgiveness from another person or directly from God. In order to have remorse, we must first admit that we are at fault for what is wrong. The next step is to move toward making amends. Sometimes only a nudging guilt will finally get us to concede our transgression and ask for pardon. Our culture encourages covering up guilt, turning away from self-reprisal and putting the blame for misdeeds onto someone or something else. I recall hearing a woman on the news explain her action this way: "I didn't really steal the neighbor's dog. I just didn't return it." If we continually deny or place the blame for our misdeeds elsewhere, we slip into a pattern where we rationalize our failures away by telling ourselves it really isn't our fault. The opposite pattern of hanging onto guilt and continually promoting self-blame, of course, is not healthy either.

How do we deal with guilt? Check to see if it's valid. If so, acknowledge the misbehavior. Ask for forgiveness. Then, let go of the guilty feeling and resolve to go forward to be our best self.

 Grant me honesty of mind and heart, God, so I can acknowledge my failures and wrongdoings.

120

Awaiting Something Glorious

The sufferings of this present time are as nothing compared with the glory to be revealed for us.

ROMANS
8:18

How difficult to keep a positive perspective when we are overcome with pain and difficulties. Who cares about "the glory to be revealed" when we are full of aches and woes! The eventual freedom from suffering promised to us when we pass from this life to the next may seem far away. We may find it impossible to say "my sufferings are as nothing." At most, we might be able to accept that the current pain will not last forever.

Faith sustains us when suffering overwhelms us, assuring us there is more to life than what we experience. What we suffer now is part of our purification, bringing about our spiritual transformation, drawing us into a closer union with God, leading us toward the mystery of what is yet to be revealed.

At times like this it helps to keep our hearts focused on the Christ who became like us, who suffered immensely, and who was raised from the dead. This Risen One is our Mentor in Hope. Let us not give up nor give in to despair or utter desolation when we are suffering. Instead, let us lean on the strength of the Holy One and trust that there is "something glorious" awaiting us beyond our experience of the present situation.

 Mentor of Hope, comfort and strengthen each person in pain of any kind.

See and Accept Your Goodness

Since we have gifts that differ according to the grace given to us, let us exercise them.

ROMANS 12:6

Have you ever heard people say, "Oh, I am just a..." and then describe themselves in a way that makes them sound insignificant? Sometimes the comment slips out without their realizing it. I've heard things like "I'm just a housewife," "just a friend," "just a lay person," "just a senior citizen." The word "just" implies a limitation or defect by comparison. This kind of comment puts oneself down, indirectly saying others' gifts are more valuable, and establishes a pattern of diminishing one's own goodness.

God has created each of us as a wonderful human being with something special we are meant to share with our world. We may have our own ideas of what we think "great gifts" are, but, in reality, any and all talents have value in the eyes of God only insofar as they are developed and shared with love. Think of the simple yet significant things others have done for you that brought you great joy because they were done with kindness and consideration. If you have an "I'm just..." in you, pray to discard it. Recognize and accept the beauty of who you are in God's eyes, and do something with love today.

 Loving Creator, thank you for who I am and for how I can serve you.

An All-Inclusive Love

You shall love the Lord, your God, with all your heart, and with all your soul, and with all your strength.

DEUTERONOMY
6:5

That tiny three-letter word "all" challenges me most about the great commandment. This little word implies a totality of my love, giving of myself completely to God. I "gulp" when I think about the entirety of my self being included. "All" means every part of me, nothing left out, no holding back.

If I could do this by some sort of direct approach to God, without including the requirement to love other people, I might be able to live that commandment quite well. How much less demanding to extend my love to God in a general way than to love God in a specific way by loving other human beings. Yet God dwells in each person, so the "all" of my love must include each one of them. The belligerent, immoral, cantankerous, offensive people are the ones who make that word "all" such a challenge.

How much more difficult to include an irritable person in my heart than to sit in meditation extending love directly to God, without any of "those people" around. Nevertheless, if I am to live the great commandment, then I simply must love everyone who bears the imprint of God within them. This obviously includes everyone.

 I desire to love you with all my heart, Beloved God. Each day I will try my best to do so.

Everything Has Been Taken from Me

He emptied himself...

PHILIPPIANS 2:7

Paul summarizes the extensive suffering of Jesus with "he emptied himself." The harshness of Jesus' passion and death took everything away from him. He was deprived of comfort, betrayed, abandoned, and filled with an agonizing depletion of self when he vulnerably yielded to the forces that betrayed and crucified him. When Jesus hung on the cross his mission and message appeared to have been a total failure.

People caught in pain-filled life events also experience this emptying process. A woman on retreat described her heartache using words that echoed Scripture: "I am being emptied. I feel I have little left inside. I can only try to live one day at a time and trust God with the future. God seems far from me. I seem far from myself. I am totally bereft with the suicide of my daughter. I feel everything has been taken from me."

Many people's pain mirrors the emptying of Jesus. Perhaps we, or someone we know, are now being emptied of what has given us love, comfort, joy, security, and support. When "emptying" takes over our life, it is surely time to unite with the strength and courage of Jesus, as this grieving mother did. In doing so, we know that we are not alone in what we experience.

 Divine Consoler, I bring to you those who are being emptied. Remind them that they are not alone.

124

The Sweet and the Sour

It will turn your stomach sour, but in your mouth it will taste as sweet as honey.

REVELATION
10:9

The verse from the Book of Revelation sounds like an advertisement for acid indigestion. Instead, it is a significant metaphor of God's promises and longings for us. In this passage, a messenger of the divine holds a scroll that is to be eaten. The scroll's sweetness symbolizes the benefits to those who follow God's ways, but the scroll is also sour because it contains the promise of suffering that goes with the demanding journey of living our lives well.

This strong truth is applicable to our lives in varied ways. Rarely do loving benefits come to fruition without some suffering and struggle. Parents know this all too well when they try to balance discipline of their children with loving companionship. Pastors who value their ministry experience the hardships that come with endless hours of commitments. Those in recovery from addictions suffer the challenge of remaining sober and drug-free. The successful person often bears the burden of being too busy. The honest person may have less financially, but more peace of mind. None of us gets off without some sour stomach when we taste the sweet honey of living in a way pleasing to God.

 Loving God, as I seek the spiritual benefits your enduring presence offers me, may I also accept the cost of receiving these wonderful gifts.

Encouraging Kindness

And he came down quickly and received him with joy.
LUKE
19:6

I am amazed at the courage of Zacchaeus. If I had been in that tree and my eavesdropping was discovered, I would have been humbled into silence—too ashamed or befuddled to be a host for the person at whom I'd been trying to sneak a peek. Not Zacchaeus! He is delighted by the opportunity and hurries down from his perch to take Jesus to his home immediately, ready to give him gracious hospitality.

Imagine the welcoming love exuded through the presence of Jesus, powerful enough to give the man in the tree so much self-confidence and enthusiasm. Jesus first let Zacchaeus know he valued him enough to want to spend time with him. The rich tax collector sensed this kindness and was immediately drawn to change his sinful ways in order to be the kind of person that the presence of Jesus inspired. On the spot, Zacchaeus turns his heart toward a changed behavior because Jesus sees the good in him and tells him so by asking to stay at his house.

Unfortunately, I tend to see the sinfulness first and never get around to extending openness and kindness. The Gospel today reminds me that when I am busy judging others, I easily lose sight of their basic goodness.

 Jesus, so many people are waiting to come to the home of my heart. I pray that I may invite them as lovingly as you invited Zacchaeus.

Our Heart Knows the Right Thing

The law of the Lord is perfect, refreshing the soul.

PSALM
19:8

How can something like a law refresh the soul? Rules, regulations, policies, commandments, and other aspects of the "law" sound cold and drab but, in reality, living by good norms leads to a life of energizing strength. Individuals live by external laws (political, social, religious) as well as internal laws determined by their conscience and experienced faith. When the external and internal laws fit together, an individual receives the energizing freedom that allows engagement in life without spiritual discordance.

I experience the refreshment described in Psalm 19 each time I choose to do what I know in my heart of hearts is the "right thing" to do. I particularly receive this refreshment when I choose to do something that I do not especially want to do, but realize I must do in order to live as a person of integrity. When what I believe matches what I do, a quiet satisfaction and a gentle peace stirs in my soul. An example of this is when I want to repeat something negative I have been told about another person. If I listen to my "inner law" I know that I need to keep those comments to myself. If I do so, I recognize right away that my choice is a good one. I sense a refreshing satisfaction and a renewed intent to be a person of genuine love.

 Refresh my spirit with your law of love, O God.

Giving from Our Ample Poverty

Those others have all made offerings from their surplus wealth, but she, from her poverty, has offered her whole livelihood.

LUKE
21:4

There are numerous ways we can be like the impoverished widow who gave from her meager resources. We do this not only when we struggle financially, but anytime we lack the fullness of what is needed to give to God and others. When we have bodily aches and pains, we can go beyond them and give our cheerfulness. If we feel inadequate in expressing our sorrow, we can still go to the grieving and bring the compassion of our physical presence. We may feel emotionally drained, but we can bring whatever meager energy we have to someone in need of our loving care.

When we experience the poverty of not feeling God's presence, we can still give ourselves to God through prayer. If we think we do not have excess time from our schedule to spare for anyone else, we can reach beyond our self and choose to give the necessary time. When something given or done for us does not totally meet our expectations, we can still offer a word of praise or gratitude. Yes, there are many ways we can be the widow who gave from her poverty.

 Dear God, teach me how to give from my poverty when life requires a response of giving from me. Help me to reach beyond my meagerness to the ample supply of your grace.

Sharing Abundance

I know indeed how to live in humble circumstances; I know also how to live with abundance.

PHILIPPIANS 4:12

Paul thanked the Philippians for their generosity and assured them he was at peace with having much or having little. Are you surprised that Paul mentioned being able to live with "abundance"? He makes an apt point because some people find it more difficult to live with abundance than with scarcity. Every once in awhile I hear comments like: "Oh, that's too good for me" or "I'm the one who should be giving" or "I can't accept this when I know there's so much poverty in the world." We make a mistake in not accepting the abundance of life when it comes our way. Our rejection lessens our gratitude.

Jesus never preached against abundance. Rather, he taught that those who have plenty are required to share their plenitude. A gift accepted gratefully brings joy to the giver. Each of us knows how it feels when we are the one doing the giving. It takes a certain humility to enjoy the bounty others provide for us out of their generosity and goodness. Every person in the world deserves kindness and abundance. Let us be at peace whether we are the one giving or the one receiving. And let us be grateful for whatever we have, be it an abundance or a scarcity.

 Giver of Gifts, thank you most of all for the abundance of your love.